The Self-Taught Agile Tester

A Step-By-Step Guide to Learn
Agile Testing Using a Real-Life Project

Chhavi Raj Dosaj

The Self-Taught Agile Tester: A Step-By-Step Guide to Learn Agile Testing Using a Real-Life Project

By Chhavi Raj Dosaj

Contents

About the Book

This book will help you to learn how testing is done in Agile software development. A little prior knowledge of software testing will help, but it is not a pre-requisite. This book is divided into two main sections. The first part of the book provides a detailed explanation of all the topics relevant to understand Agile software development, and this section will help you to understand the following:

- Why we need Agile software development
- Agile Manifesto and principles
- Different Agile approaches
- Agile team structure
- Difference between Traditional and Agile testing
- How requirements are managed in Agile projects
- Different Agile Ceremonies
- Estimation and Automation in Agile projects
- How quality risks are managed in Agile projects
- Tools used by Agile teams

The second half focuses on a step-by-step walk-through of a real-world Agile testing project. This knowledge will help you understand how different processes and ceremonies are run from the initiation until the end in the Agile projects and how the Agile tester participates and contributes to them.

The book provides details of each project activity, which will help you understand how the test activities are planned, executed, and monitored in real Agile projects. This book will help you learn Agile testing and will guide you when working as an Agile tester on a real project. It will teach you everything you should know about Agile software testing with references to a real-life project and help you secure a job as an Agile tester.

In this book, the word "Agile" is used in a broad sense, and most of the principles and practices discussed in the book are applicable for Scrum, Kanban, XP, and other Agile approaches.

If you are new to testing, you may find some of the topics too technical. My advice is to skim through these topics and move forward. Once you have finished the entire book you can revisit them, by the time these topics will be easier to understand.

Acknowledgments

I would like to thank my colleagues from the Reserve Bank of Australia for helping me with the book.

Sandeep Jain- Solution Architect for the solution design diagrams for IMT project,

Hari Yagnamurthy- Senior Business Analyst for helping me with the creation of user stories for the IMT project,

Anna Douderina- UI designer for creating the wireframes for the IMT project web pages,

Arun Sree Kumar for creating the diagrams for the book

Disclaimer

Although all efforts have been made to ensure the accuracy of this book's contents, we cannot guarantee 100% correctness of the information contained herein.

If you find any factual anomalies, grammar, or spelling errors, please send it along with your comments and suggestions to the author.

1 Why we need Agile Software Development

Since 1970 all the software's were developed using a traditional Waterfall model, which follows a linear, sequential design approach where progress flows downwards in one direction, like a Waterfall. So why was there a need for another software development approach like Agile?

Consider the below case study to compare Waterfall software development with Agile software development.

A bank is planning to build a new mobile app for their customers with the following set of features:

- **Feature A** – Customer can change ATM card PIN.
- **Feature B** – Customer can cancel and request replacement ATM cards.
- **Feature C** – Customer can check their Accounts Transaction History.
- **Feature D** – Customer can change Account daily payment Limits.
- **Feature E** – Customer can Block and Unblock lost cards.

The bank has started a new project to successfully deliver this mobile app and wants to choose between Waterfall and Agile software development. First, if they have decided to go with the Waterfall model, the project will go through the following stages.

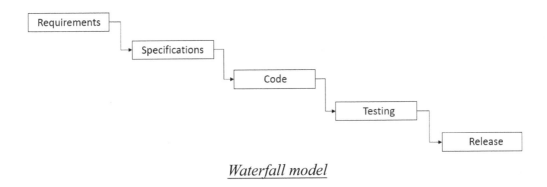

Waterfall model

In the Waterfall model, the project is delivered through a set of phases, as shown in the diagram above. These phases are completed one after another. If a particular phase is not completed and approved, advancing to the next step or any later phase is not possible.

In this model, test activities only occur after all other development activities have been completed.

These are the high-level activities that will take place as part of developing the bank app:

Requirements phase

In this phase, the Business or System Analysts will gather the requirements for all the features (**A+B+C+D+E**) from the customer or their representatives (business team). These requirements will be documented as part of the user requirement document, which will define the project's scope. After the project starts, if the customer requests any changes to this agreed scope, it has to go through a lengthy change request process which can affect the overall project effort and delivery dates.

Specification/Analysis phase

In this phase, based on the user requirements, the business analyst will create the specification documents, i.e., business requirement document (BRD), covering all the functional and non-functional requirements for all the app features. The architect or solution designer will define the technical design or architecture for the solution, which will cover all the functions identified in the specification document. Based on the specification and design documents testing team can start preparing the high-level test cases. Meanwhile, the development team can start creating component specification documents based on the design & specification documents which will be used as the basis for coding activities.

Development phase

During this phase, the developers will code different components of the mobile app based on the component specifications to meet the required functional and non-functional attributes. After the development the developers will carry out unit and unit integration testing for these components of the mobile app. Meanwhile, the testing team will create detailed low-level test cases based on the high-level scenarios prepared earlier and trace them back to the requirements to ensure sufficient coverage. They will also ensure the test environment and test data is ready.

Testing Phase

During this phase, the development team will deploy the complete mobile app to the testing environment, and the testing team will start executing the test cases to test all the features. There will be ST, SIT, UAT test phases to ensure all the features are working according to the specifications. After all the testing is complete, the mobile app can be released to the production environment so the end-user can use it.

Now, based on the chosen team size, the high-level effort required for each phase is as follows:

- Requirement gathering activities– 1 month
- Analysis/specification activities- 1 month
- Development activities - 2 months
- Testing & release activity – 2 months

So, roughly after six months, the team will be able to deliver the mobile app to the end-user. If the customer requires any changes during the project, it can delay the delivery dates.

Let us now analyse the **drawbacks** of using the Waterfall approach for our mobile app project.

Makes changes difficult

For our app development project, the first time the business team or potential user group will see the app's working version is during the UAT testing phase, which is almost after five months the project is started.

During these five months, it is highly likely that some of these requirements may require changes due to internal and external reasons. What if the users are not satisfied with the app after running the UAT scenarios and ask for changes? Incorporating these changes at such a late stage will require a lot of rework in specifications, development, and testing, which will delay the overall delivery to the end-user by a few more months.

Thus, this methodology leaves almost very little room for unexpected changes during the project release in its traditional form.

Late and unpredictable delivery

Using Waterfall methodology, the bank has to wait for a minimum of six months to launch the app. If the bank wants to launch a simple app with a minimum set of features as soon as possible to make their customer happy and keep up with its competitors. In sequential development, however, this is not possible as there is no option for a phase-wise delivery of features. Also, if one of the phases is delayed or there are any major issues found during testing, it can make the delivery date unpredictable.

Delays testing until after completion

As the testing team waits for the whole product to be ready before starting the dynamic testing, the test execution starts very late in the Waterfall model. In our case of the mobile app, it is almost four months after the start of the project. This increases the chances of technical risks; if any major issues are found during test execution that require rework, it can delay the delivery dates.

Lack of customer involvement

As we have seen, other than requirement gathering, there is very less involvement of the customer or their representatives in different project phases, leaving no room for their feedback. It is difficult and challenging to develop a product without active customer involvement in today's changing market environment.

No room for innovation

The Waterfall model is not flexible enough to bring changes to the project. This makes it difficult for new ideas to be welcomed and included in the product.

There are, however, few advantages of using the Waterfall model, such as:

Simple and Clear structure

It is intuitive and simple to understand. All are phases are in sequential order. There are specific deliverables for each phase. This methodological approach offers a simple structure for any new team members to follow and understand.

Clear information transfer

In the sequential software development, there is a lot of emphasis on documentation; therefore, heavy documents are created to support each project activity. The information transfer between different phases and between the teams is easy, especially when the team is not co-located. But this heavy documentation also increases the project team effort.

As we can see, the drawback overweighs the advantages that Waterfall offers, and that is why people started looking for alternatives. Let's now use **Agile software development** (iterative and incremental software development) for this app development project. But before that, it is important to understand the iterative and incremental development independently.

In iterative development, the project progress through a number of successive refinements. The development team develops a first cut of the system; this may be incomplete or weak in some areas. The team then iteratively refines those areas until the product is satisfactory. With each iteration, the software is improved through the addition of greater detail.

For example, in the first iteration, the team will code the transaction screen to support only the recent ten transactions history. In the second iteration, the team will work on the functionality to add multiple pages for transactions. Finally, a third iteration will add transaction filter functionality.

In **incremental development**, the software is built and delivered in pieces. Each piece, or increment, represents a complete subset of functionality. The increment may be either small or large, perhaps ranging from just a system's login screen on the small end to a highly flexible set of data management screens.

For example, the team will fully analyse, fully code, and test the transaction history functionality. This feature will be released to the customer, and other features will be delivered incrementally.

Agile development is **both iterative and incremental**. They are iterative because the work of one iteration can be improved upon in subsequent iterations. They are incremental because completed work is delivered throughout the project. In Agile development, similar to sequential model the same requirement analysis, development, and testing phases are there but for small pieces of work items, as we will see now.

- The team will break the features into a number of user stories, which are a general explanation of a software feature but written from the end-user's perspective.
- These stories are then added to the product backlog with priority, so the team is aware of the overall work.
- The whole project will be divided into small iterations, which can be 2-4 weeks duration.
- In each iteration, the team will pick the user stories from the backlog based on the priority, which can be developed, tested, and delivered independently.
- There will be a customer representative working with the project team from the start of the project till the end. They are called Product Owners in Agile projects. It is their responsibility to explain the requirement/features to the team, assign priority to the requirements/features, and collaborate with the team to clarify or further refine the requirement.

The team will spend an initial iteration, which can be longer than the normal iteration on the initial setup and overall planning activities, including:

- Deciding on the scope of the project
- Creating an initial system architecture
- Breaking the features into user stories
- Adding these stories with priority to the product backlog
- Setting the environment for development and testing activity
- Procuring necessary tools required for project execution

Once the initial iteration is completed, the team can start fixed-length iterations where the team can pick the user stories from the product backlog based on the priority. During these iterations, the team will analyze, develop, and test these stories with help from the Product Owner. Once these activities are completed for a feature, they can be released to the end-users.

Following diagram shows how different features will be developed in Agile methodology.

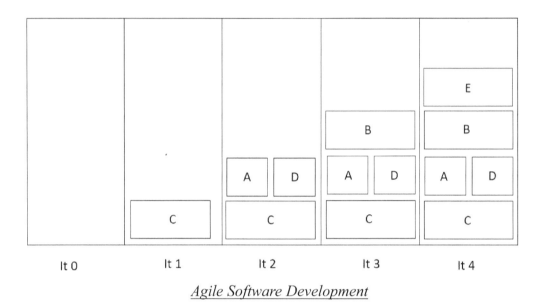

Agile Software Development

In this case, we can see there are many advantages of using Agile development as compared to Waterfall development:

Early and Predictable Delivery

Agile development allows the release of the Minimal Viable Product (MVP) as soon as possible to the market. If the bank wants to release the app with just the "Transaction history" feature, it is possible only using Agile development. For this feature development, if the team spends three weeks on the initial iteration and then the next two iterations (two weeks size) on the stories; by the end of seven weeks, the app will be ready for the end-user compared to 26 weeks (six months) in Waterfall.

The subsequent features can also be released soon as the team has already done the setup and planning in the initial iteration.

Enables early and frequent feedback from customer

In the Waterfall model, the customer representative is able to see the single finished product quite late in the development lifecycle. At this point, if there is any customer feedback, it is often too late for the development team to address that effectively.

In contrast, Agile projects have short iterations; at the end of each iteration, workable software with limited functionality is demonstrated to the customer. This enables the project team to receive early and continuous feedback on product quality.

Early and frequent feedback helps the team focus on the features with the highest business value, and these are delivered to the customer first.

High chance of product fulfilling the customer needs

The customer representative (Product Owner collaborates with the team in requirement reviews, planning, and testing activities from the start of the project until the end and provides feedback at regular intervals. Also, in each iteration, the team demo the working software to the Product Owner and wider audience; therefore, it is very likely the software will meet the customer needs.

Allowing for Frequent Changes

As the team focuses on delivering an agreed product's features during each iteration, there is an opportunity to refine and reprioritize the overall product backlog constantly. New or changed backlog items can be planned for the next iteration, providing the opportunity to introduce changes within a few weeks.

During the project, if the bank finds that changes are required for a feature, they can add the changes easily to the product backlog rather than going through a lengthy process of the change request.

Focuses on Users

In Agile, the requirements (user stories are defined from the user perspective, allowing the team to understand what business value each story brings, which can help them in the development and testing activity. User stories are discussed in chapter 5.

Focuses on Business Value

Agile development allows the customer or their representative to decide the priority of features during the project. The team is flexible, understands what's most important to the customer, and can work and deliver the most business value features first.

During the project, if the bank finds high demand for one of the features, they can increase the priority of the stories related to that feature, and the team will pick them for development in the next iteration.

Improves Quality

By breaking down the project into manageable units, the project team can focus on high-quality development, testing, and collaboration. This will allow producing frequent builds and conducting testing and reviews during each iteration. This approach improves the quality as the defects are found and fixed quickly, and any expectation mismatches are identified earlier in the project lifecycle.

Transparency

In Agile projects all the team members, including the customers representatives are involved in all the project activities. The progress is shared with all the team member in daily stand-up meeting. Thus, the work in progress is transparent to all the stakeholders.

Looking at the case study, it is clear that in the current business environment where more and more projects are subjected to changes due to legislation, competitor activity, and technology advances, Agile software development is more suitable. Moreover, if time-to-market is important for the project, it can only be achieved using Agile development.

In the next few sections, we will go through Agile development's details and see how it differs from traditional sequential development.

2 Agile Manifesto and principles

Origin Story

In early 2001, a group of individuals, representing the most widely used lightweight software development methodologies, came across to discuss their work and look for any common themes in their various approaches. The group members shared their views on the current software development state and discussed how it could be improved.

They agreed that the problem was due to the fact that most of the companies were so focused on excessively planning and documenting their software development cycles that they lost sight of what really mattered the most for the successful project—satisfying their customers.

Together they proposed a new way of developing software "by doing it and helping others do it." They agreed on a common set of values and principles, which became the Manifesto for Agile Software Development or the Agile Manifesto [**http://agilemanifesto.org**/]

Agile Manifesto

The Agile Manifesto, which provides a cornerstone for all Agile methods, contains four statements of values:

- Individuals and interactions **Ov ER** processes and tools
- Working software **Ov ER** comprehensive documentation
- Customer collaboration **Ov ER** contract negotiation
- Responding to change **Ov ER** following a plan

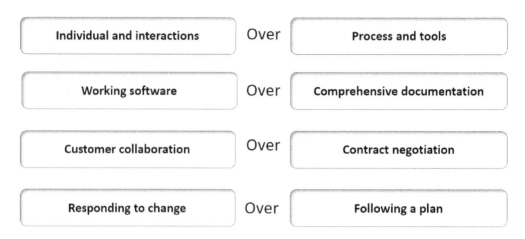

The Manifesto of Agile Software Development

The Agile Manifesto does not suggest replacing the items in the right with the left; rather, it stresses prioritizing left items over right.

Individuals and Interactions

Agile development argues that there are benefits for the project which use good tools and processes. However, over-reliance on these tools and/or processes subsequently results in rigidity that does not cope well, especially when there are changes required to the project. As it is the people who produce software, teams can work most effectively through direct communication and interactions rather than over-relying on tools or processes.

Teams who frequently interact with each other rather than rigidly following the process are proven more effective in software development.

Note
• Agile development is people-centered
• The Agile team is composed of a small number of team members who possess different skill sets
• The interaction between the team members is close and frequent
• Emphasis is on collaboration among team members rather than rigidly following the processes and over-reliance on tools

Working Software

In Agile development, working software with reduced functionality is available much early in the software development lifecycle. From a customer perspective, working software is much more useful and valuable than detailed documentation. It allows providing rapid feedback to the development team and can offer business benefits much earlier.

Working software also helps the customers as they are often unsure about what they want until they can see a limited working prototype. This approach is beneficial when the problem areas are new and unclear.

Note
• In Agile development, the focus is to develop working software regularly and frequently, ideally at the end of each iteration.
• Working system is more useful for the customers than detailed documentation and enables them to provide quick feedback to the development team
• Agile development can confer significant time-to-market advantage due to working software available early
• Working software is helpful where the customer is not clear about the solutions and problem areas
• It helps in bringing innovation in new problem domains

Customer Collaboration

In traditional development approaches, as soon as the project's requirements and scope are confirmed with the customer, contracts are formed, and the team follows that for software development delivery. During the initial phase, customers often find great difficulty in specifying system requirements, and then in the later phase, they are subjected to negotiating the contracts.

Collaborating directly with the customer improves the likelihood of understanding exactly what the customer requires and results in customer satisfaction. Having contracts with customers may be important but having regular and close collaboration with them is likely to bring more success to the project.

Note
• Customers may find it difficult to describe the exact and accurate requirements for a system during the initial stages
• Collaborating directly with the customer helps to understand the expectations correctly and increases the success of the project
• In Agile development, contracts with customers are not set in the center of attention

Responding to Change

The environment in which the business operates, such as legislation, competitor activity, technology advances, and other factors, can have significant influences on the project. To simply ignore this and produce a detailed rigid plan in the early stages of project development is not useful.

If changes are enviable in software development, then it is better to accept the fact and create processes that cope well with change. Agile accommodates these factors in the development process and encourages initial light planning based on the current level of detail. It promotes flexibility in work practices to embrace changes rather than adhering rigidly to a plan.

Note
• Software projects are subject to change due to internal and external changes
• Changes have a strong impact on the project and the development process should quickly respond to these changes
• Agile teams are **expected to anticipate and welcome change** throughout the life cycle

Agile Principles

The core Agile Manifesto values are captured in twelve principles, they are:

1. **Our highest priority is to satisfy the customer through the early and continuous delivery of valuable software**.

   In the current environment, the customers look for early delivery of software rather than waiting for it for long; therefore, Agile teams should strive to deliver the Minimal Viable Product (MVP) as early as possible and improve upon it at regular intervals. Each new version of the software adds additional features to the previously developed version.

2. **Welcome changing requirements, even late in development. Agile processes harness change for the customer's competitive advantage**.

In Agile projects, as the working software is ready early, it helps the customer better understand what they want and provide feedback in the form of changes. Therefore, the team should consider changes as a positive sign. If the team welcomes these changes even late during the development, the software will satisfy the customer's current and latest needs and give them a competitive advantage over others.

3. **Deliver working software frequently, at intervals between a few weeks to a few months, with a preference for the shorter timescale.**

Agile projects have short iterations, preferably at the end of few iterations working software is delivered to the customer. This enables the project team to receive early and continuous feedback on the solution.

4. **Business people and developers must work together daily throughout the project.**

In traditional projects, the software development team is often isolated from the business people. In contrast, in Agile projects there is continuous involvement of the business people in all the team activities on a daily basis throughout the course of the project. From the start of the project, these business people are involved in all team activities. This helps find any gaps in requirements early, and getting regular feedback from business people helps produce successful outcomes.

5. **Build projects around motivated individuals. Give them the environment and support they need and trust them to get the job done**.

The people working on the project are the key to the success of the Agile project. The team will succeed if they are empowered to make decisions and provided necessary support in removing any impediments to productivity.

With the correct coaching, environment, and tools, motivated team members will feel enabled to do their work.

6. **The most efficient and effective method of conveying information to and within a development team is face-to-face conversation.**

Technology has increased the number of ways in which humans can communicate. In most projects, team members use email, phone, chat, video as a means of conversation, but none of these are as good as a face-to-face conversation. This is one of the reasons Agile promotes co-location.

7. **Working software is the primary measure of progress.**

As software projects can take a long time to deliver, it is necessary to measure the progress at regular intervals. In traditional projects, phase completion is used as a measure for project progress; in contrast, in Agile projects, at the end of each iteration team delivers working software that is used to measure the progress of the project.

8. **Agile processes promote sustainable development. The sponsors, developers, and users should be able to maintain a constant pace indefinitely.**

Agile projects aim for a sustainable pace for development that minimizes overtime and excessive hours for the team members. It helps in high-quality work as the team members are motivated; also, there is a reduction in the number of mistakes and omissions in the project as team members are not under continual pressure.

9. **Continuous attention to technical excellence and good design enhances agility.**

If teams neglect a good technical design for too long, their speed and time-to-market will start to slow down in the long run. Therefore, the Agile team should use good design techniques from the start to achieve a high-quality end product that requires a focus on quality all the way through development.

10. **Simplicity—the art of maximizing the amount of work not done—is essential.**

Developing only the solution required to achieve the project goal is the key factor in Agile projects. The Agile team does not incorporate every potential future requirement or possible request in the initial design. Instead, they focus on making the design as simple as possible. Thus, if the customer wishes to add a new feature, this request can be easily accommodated. For example, once the Product Owner has decided what elements need to be built into the product, they should be categorized into "must-have" or "nice to have." The team should first focus only on the "must-have" features.

11. **The best architectures, requirements, and designs emerge from self- organizing teams.**

The Agile team is empowered to self-organize and decides how best to achieve project objectives without any fears. The sense of team ownership helps in taking responsibility and accountability for the project and enables motivation and healthy communication for any new ideas.

12. **At regular intervals, the team reflects on how to become more effective, then tunes and adjusts its behavior accordingly.**

At regular intervals, Agile teams engage in self-reflection. They examine what is working and what is not working and adjust accordingly. They can identify issues and then take action to improve the process. This principle makes the team successful by not accepting the status-quo but always looking to improve the situation.

There are different Agile approaches, but all of them use different practices to put these values and principles into action.

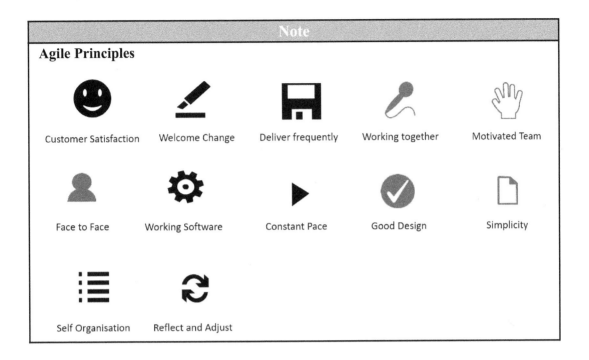

Note

Agile Principles

Customer Satisfaction   Welcome Change   Deliver frequently   Working together   Motivated Team

Face to Face   Working Software   Constant Pace   Good Design   Simplicity

Self Organisation   Reflect and Adjust

3 | **Different Agile Approaches**

While there are many implementations of Agile methodologies, the most common phases in all of them are discovery, preparation of product backlog, and working on these backlog items in iterations. We will discuss these in detail below:

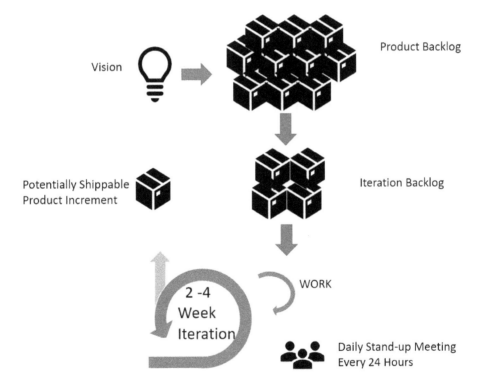

Discovery phase

Before starting any new project, the team must understand the end-user problem they are trying to solve. When the team is aware of the user, their challenges, needs, and wants, they can understand the vision and gain insights into different aspects of the problem.

This is why the project using Agile software development starts with a series of discovery sessions to understand the customers' goals, challenges, and business environment. These sessions include key members of the Agile project team discussing the key project goals with the customer to ensure that the team clearly understands the customer requirements.

Preparing the Product Backlog

During the Discovery phase, the team works together to create a high-level wish list of all the software features required to fulfill the customer's need. The team works with the customer to prioritize these features, determining the order in which the features are elaborated, developed, tested, and delivered. By allowing the customer to prioritize, the team stays focused on delivering the highest value features before moving on to lower value features.

Iterations

After ensuring the team understands the customer's vision and has created a high-level backlog of features, the team delivers features through a series of time-boxed iterations. These iterations are fixed durations of 1-4 weeks. The duration of iteration is selected based on number of factors like project size, risk, complexity etc. In each iteration, the team creates and delivers the iteration backlog which is a subset of the overall product backlog.

Continuing the Cycle

These iterations are continued to deliver additional features and incorporate feedback from previous iterations. Each successive iteration provides improvements to work completed in previous iterations and adds new features to the system.

As the software's features grow incrementally, it is important to ensure that the tested and delivered features in the earlier iterations are still working fine. This is the reason regression testing is important in Agile development.

Different Agile Software Development Approaches

Different Agile approaches implement the values and principles of the Agile Manifesto in different ways. Some of the common Agile approaches are Scrum, Kanban, Extreme Programming (XP).

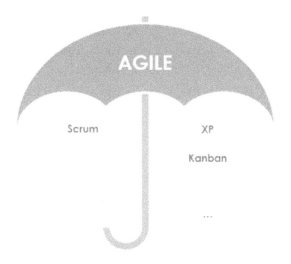

Different Agile Development Approaches

This book covers Scrum and Kanban, which are the two most popular and commonly used approaches for software development.

SCRUM

Scrum is one of the most popular Agile software development approach and is most suitable for greenfield projects. Scrum terms and concepts, such as Sprint and Product Owner, have become part of the de facto language of Agile. At a high-level Scrum constituent, the following instruments and practices:

- **Sprint**: Scrum divides a project into iterations, called sprints. Sprints are of fixed length (usually two to four weeks) for the entire project.

- **Product Increment**: Each sprint results in a potentially releasable/ shippable product (called an increment).

- **Product Backlog**: The Product Owner manages a prioritized list of planned product items (called the product backlog). The product backlog evolves from sprint to sprint; this activity is known as backlog refinement.

- **Sprint Backlog**: At the start of each sprint, the Scrum team selects a set of highest priority items from the product backlog. Collectively, these items will form the sprint backlog. This way of working is based on the "**pull**" principle because the Scrum team selects the items from the sprint in contrast to the Product Owner "**pushing**" items to the team.

- **Definition of Done**: All functionality or features will have associated acceptance criteria used to verify correctness. However, to be complete and shippable, a piece of software will probably have to satisfy other criteria such as being adequately documented and written to an agreed standard. The Scrum team discusses and defines appropriate criteria for sprint completion. This discussion creates a deeper level of understanding of the backlog items and product requirements. It helps the team to be clear about what constitutes "Done" and deliver a potentially releasable product at each sprint's end.

- **Time-boxing**: In Scrum, time-boxing not only fixes the duration of the sprints in a release but also applies to a variety of other activities such as meeting start and end times. Time-boxing sprints mean that only those tasks team believes can be finished within the sprint become part of the sprint backlog. If the team cannot complete a task within a sprint, the associated product features are moved back into the product backlog.

- **Transparency**: The team reports and updates sprint status on a daily basis in a meeting called the **Daily Scrum**. Interested stakeholders can join the meeting to observe the team's progress. Also, the team uses a task board to record all the tasks progress, which is visible to all the team members. This makes the current sprint's content and progress, including test results, visible to the team, management, and all interested parties.

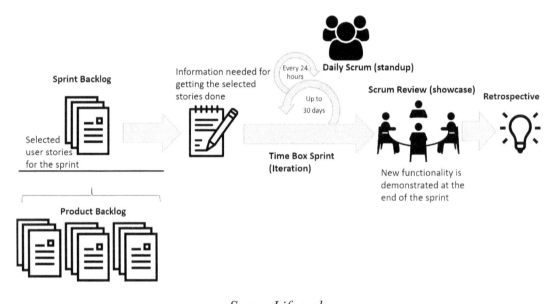

Scrum Lifecycle

KANBAN

Kanban is another Agile approach that is particularly suited when the team has a steady stream of similar work or tasks. The general objective is to visualize and optimize the flow of work within a value-added chain. Kanban helps manage the project by limiting the 'work in progress' to regularly and consistently deliver value to users. Kanban seeks to make the value-adding process visible so that any problems in the flow of value (bottlenecks, delays, wasting effort, etc.) can be seen and addressed.

Kanban utilizes three instruments:

- **Kanban Board**: Kanban board is used to visualize the value chain to be managed. Each column shows a station, which is a set of related activities, e.g., development or testing. The items to be produced or tasks to be completed are symbolized as tickets and placed in the Kanban board's far-left column. In this way, the tickets are seen to be part of the backlog. Tickets move from left to right across the board through the stations. Kanban boards are widely used in software development to make the workflow visible.

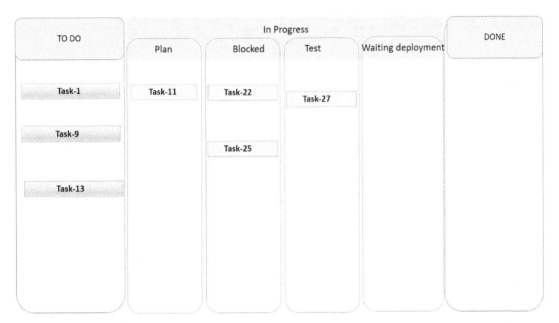

Example of Kanban Board

- **Work-in-Progress Limit**: The amount of parallel active tasks is strictly limited. This is controlled by the maximum number of tickets allowed for a station and/or globally for the board. Whenever a station has the free capacity, the team member pulls a ticket from the predecessor station.

- **Lead Time:** Lead time is the amount of time it takes for a unit of work to travel through the team's workflow–from the moment work starts till it is shipped. Kanban is used to optimize the continuous flow of tasks by minimizing the (average) lead time for the complete value stream.

The following table displays the similarities and differences between Scrum and Kanban.

	Scrum	k anban
Release methodology	At the end of each sprint	Continuous delivery or at the team's discretion
v isualization of tasks	Task boards	Kanban Board
Time-boxing (Iterations or sprints)	Mandatory; Shippable product at the end of the sprint	Optional; releasing deliverables item by item
k ey metrics	Velocity	Lead time

4 | Agile Team

Agile team compromise of different team members who possess the diverse skill set and take different roles; at a high level, we can categorize them into two, customer and development teams.

Customer Team:

The customer team includes the Product Owner, business SME's, business analysts representing the project's business side and guides the development team on what is important to deliver.

The customer team understands the customer, their needs and business, and has a clear vision of the value the team is delivering to the customer. Therefore, they set the priority for work and ensure that the team is delivering the most value to the customer. The customer team also balances the needs of other stakeholders in the organization.

In Scrum, the Product Owner represents the customer, prepares the user stories for the product backlog, and decides on acceptance criteria with the help of the business analyst.

Following responsibilities lies with the customer team:

1. **Defining the vision-** They define the goals and create a roadmap for the project. They are responsible for making sure the goals are clear for the team, and the vision is aligned with business objectives.

2. **Managing and prioritizing the product backlog -** They create the list of backlog items and prioritize them based on the overall strategy and business objectives. They will also map out any project dependencies to inform the necessary sequence of development. They are responsible for managing and continually updating it based on evolving project needs.

3. **Evaluate product progress at each iteration -**They take a primary role in inspecting and evaluating product progress through each iteration. Once they are satisfied with the story (work), **only** then it can be considered as completed (done).

Development team:

The development team comprises different kinds of people involved in the product development, including architects, solution designers, UI designers, DBA, developers, and testers. The team is self-organized and cross-functional. There is no team lead, so the whole team makes the decisions.

The 'development team' has the members who have the right skills to develop, test, and ship the product. The development team is a self-organizing team that makes decisions to get the work done.

The development team's responsibilities include:

1. **Participating in release and iteration activities -** They participate in all the release and iteration activities with the customer team and contribute based on their skillsets.

2. **Delivering the work** – Once the iteration is started, the stories are broken into a number of tasks to deliver the work. Development team members work on these tasks and provide the status to the team during the daily stand-up meetings.

Following are some of the key aspects of the Agile team which differentiate it from the traditional team:

Traditional Teams

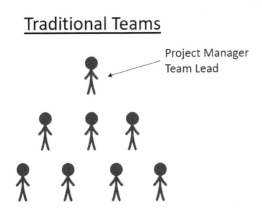

Project Manager
Team Lead

Agile Teams

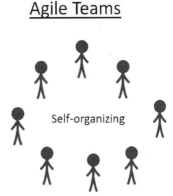

Self-organizing

- **Self-organized and cross-functional**

  As compared to traditional team, Agile team is self-organized and cross-functional. There is no concept of team lead; therefore, the whole team collectivity takes decisions. This approach promotes more effective and efficient team dynamics.

- **Whole-Team Approach**

  In Agile development, the quality of the product is not the sole responsibility of the testers, but it is the responsibility of the whole team.

  The essence of the whole-team approach lies in the testers, developers, and business representatives working together in every step of the development process. Testers work closely with both developers and the Product Owner to ensure that the desired quality levels are achieved. Testers support and collaborate with the Product Owner to help them create suitable acceptance criteria and work closely with developers to agree on the test automation approach.

  The whole team is involved in any consultations or meetings in which product features are presented, analyzed, or estimated. The concept of involving testers, developers, and the Product Owner in all feature discussions is an Agile project is known as the **power of three.**

- **Small team**

  Agile teams are relatively small, with as few as three people and as many as nine people. Ideally, the whole team shares the same workspace, as co-location strongly facilitates communication and interaction.

  With a small team, less time is spent in coordinating effort; therefore, all the team members are able to participate collectively in all the activities in Agile projects.

Note

In Scrum, there are three roles defined:

- **Scrum Master**: Ensures that Scrum practices and rules are implemented and followed and resolves any issues that are impeding team progress and preventing the team from following the practices and rules. The scrum master acts as a coach to the team, not the team leader.

- **Product Owner**: Represents the customer. The Product Owner creates, maintains, and prioritizes the product backlog. This person is also not the team leader.

- **Development Team**: Develop and test the product.

Product Owner

Development Team

Scrum Master

5 Requirement in Agile projects

In traditional sequential projects, at the start of the project, the requirements specifications are created by business analysts and validated by business stakeholders. This approach often results in low-quality specifications as customers lack insight into their real needs during the start of the project. The absence of a global vision for the system, redundant or contradictory features, and other miscommunications can further degrade the specifications. Studies have soon that poor specifications are one of the main reasons for project failure in traditional sequential development.

To address these issues, Agile development promotes having high-level requirements at the start of the project, which are further analyzed and refined during the iteration based on new information. The requirement in Agile development is divided into different categories, as shown in the below hierarchical structure.

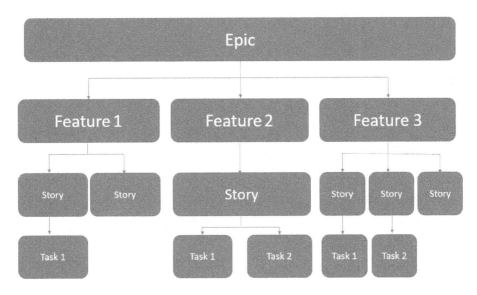

Epic -> Features -> User stories

Epic

An Epic can be defined as a high-level description of what the customer or end-user of the system wants, and accordingly, it has some value attached to it. Epic can also be called a large story, which comprises a global and a very high-level functionality of the software.

As Epics are very broad, they are usually broken down into a number of features. An epic may span multiple sprints, and multiple teams may work on these.

The epic for our bank app from chapter 1 will look like this:

"A new mobile app for the bank customer so they can use the online banking functionality on the phones."

Features/Theme

A feature or theme usually tends to describe what the software does, and broadly they can be considered as a group or collection of related user stories. The customer team defines features with the help of key customers and end-users. A feature may also span multiple sprints.

Example of features from our example of bank app from chapter 1:

- **Feature A** – Customer can change ATM card PIN.
- **Feature B** – Customer can cancel and request Replacement ATM cards.
- **Feature C** – Customer can check their Accounts Transaction History.
- **Feature D** – Customer can change Account daily payment Limits.
- **Feature E** – Customer can Block and Unblock lost cards.

The features are broken down into short individual requirements, which become user stories.

User Story

A user story is the smallest unit of work in Agile development that the team can deliver independently. It is an informal, general explanation of a software feature written from the end user's perspective. Its purpose is to articulate how a software feature will provide value to the customer. These "customers" don't have to be external end-users in the traditional sense. They can also be internal users within the organization who will be using the product.

These stories use non-technical language to provide context to the team. After reading a user story, the team knows why they are building, what they're building, and what value it creates.

Stories have **acceptance criteria** that help to define what is needed for the successful completion of that story.

User story template and examples

User stories most commonly take the following form:

As a <**role**>, I want to <**activity or capability**>

So that <**achieve some valuable outcome**>

Example from our bank app application, which we discussed in chapter 1:

As a **Banking App user,**

I want to **access my accounts Transaction History**

So that **I have a record of my expenses**

The user stories serve a number of key benefits in Agile projects:

- **Stories keep the focus on the user** – As the user story elaborates details of the small piece of a requirement that provides value for the customer, the team is able to focus on solving problems for real users.
- **Stories enable collaboration**. With the end goal defined, the team can work together to decide how best to serve the user and meet that goal.
- **Stories drive creative solutions**. Stories encourage the team to think critically and creatively about how to solve an end goal best.
- **Stories create momentum**. With each passing story, the team enjoys a small challenge and a small win, driving momentum.

Acceptance criteria (AC)

Acceptance criteria are the conditions that a software product must meet in order to be accepted by an end-user or the customer. They are unique for each story and define the feature behavior from the end-user perspective. The stories with well-written acceptance criteria help the team understand the expected outcome of the story and ensure that all stakeholders and users are satisfied with what they get.

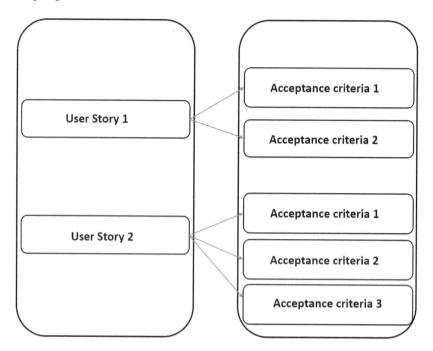

How User Stories relates to acceptance *criteria*

Acceptance criteria's help to facilitate the following purposes:

- **Defining the scope:** AC defines the boundaries of user stories. They provide precise details on functionality that helps the team understand whether the story works as expected and can be considered as completed.

- **Describing negative scenarios:** AC help defines negative scenarios and explains how the system must react to them. This helps the testers to identify what is required for testing.

- **Common understanding of the requirements**: AC synchronizes the client's visions and helps the team gain a shared understanding of the story. It enables communication within the team and helps the Product Owner answer what they need in order for this story to provide value (typically, these are the minimum functional requirements). This also helps developers know exactly what kind of behavior the feature must demonstrate.

- **Streamlining acceptance testing**: AC is the basis of the user story acceptance testing. Each acceptance criterion must be independently testable and thus have a clear pass or fail scenario. They can also be used to verify the story via automated tests. This helps the developers and testers to derive tests.

- **Helps in estimation**: AC specifies what exactly must be developed by the team. Once the team has precise requirements based on acceptance criteria, they can correctly estimate the work required to complete a particular story.

Acceptance criteria are typically written in scenario-oriented (Given/When/Then) format.

Scenario – the name for the behavior that will be described

Given – the beginning state of the scenario (**precondition**)

When – specific **action** that the user makes

Then – the outcome of the action (**result**)

When combined, these statements cover all actions that a user takes to complete a task and experience the outcome.

For the story.

As a **Banking App user,**

I want to **access my accounts Transaction History**

So that **I have a record of my expenses**

Example Acceptance criteria:

AC#1

Given the user has login to app

When the user selects the account

Then the user is shown ten recent transactions

AC#2

Given the user has login to app

When the user selects the account and clicks on page 2 of the transaction history

Then the user is shown the next ten transactions

Note
This approach for the (Given/When/Then) format is inherited from behavior-driven development (BDD) and provides a consistent structure. It provides a path that acts as a bridge to overcome the gap between the technical and the non-technical team members. The test cases are commonly written in simple English without any jargon, which is easier to understand. It also reduces the time spent on writing test cases as the system's behavior is described upfront. Therefore, this approach is encouraged in most Agile projects.

3C Concept

Ron Jefferies proposed the 3C concept to describe the component elements of a user story. The three elements are card, conversation, and confirmation:

- **Card**: The card is the physical media that describes a user story. It identifies the requirement, its criticality, and the acceptance criteria. It also includes expected development and test duration. This card is used in the product backlog, so the description should be accurate.

- **Conversation**: The requirements are communicated and understood in a number of conversations conducted between the customers, developers, and testers. The dialogue explains how the software will be used. The exchange can be documented or verbal. The tester perspective adds much to this conversation by asking questions, identifying ambiguity, missing elements such as non-functional aspects, and suggesting ways to test the story. The conversation begins during the release-planning phase and continues when the story is scheduled for inclusion in an iteration.

- **Confirmation**: The acceptance criteria discussed in the conversation are used to confirm that the story is done. These acceptance criteria cover positive and negative scenarios. To confirm that the story is done, the defined acceptance criteria should be tested and satisfied.

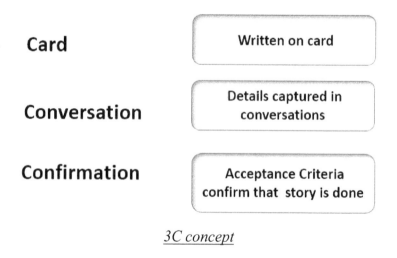

3C concept

The user stories must address both functional and non-functional characteristics. Each story includes acceptance criteria for these characteristics. These criteria should be defined in collaboration between the Product Owner, developers, and testers. This provides developers and testers with an extended vision of the feature that business representatives can validate. When a set of acceptance criteria have been satisfied, then only the Agile team considers the story as finished. The tester's unique perspective can help to improve the content and quality of user stories by identifying missing details or non-functional requirements. A tester can contribute by asking the Product Owner **open-ended questions** about the user story, **proposing ways to test the user story**, and **confirming the acceptance criteria**.

The collaborative authorship of the user story can use techniques such as brainstorming and mind mapping. To verify the user story content, the tester may also use the following **INVEST** technique:

- **I**ndependent: User story is discrete or self-contained; it is not dependent on other user stories. This is particularly important for stories that are being worked on during the same iteration since dependencies between stories during the same iteration complicate planning and prioritization.

- **N**egotiable: User story is subjected to change based on conversation within the team. The details associated with the story are worked out during this conversation.

- **V**aluable: The user story provides a business value that is clear and readily understood to everyone.

- **E**stimable: The user story needs to be clear enough for the team to be able to do an initial estimate of the story.

- **S**mall: A story has to be small enough to be completed during an iteration.

- **T**estable: The user story has clear acceptance criteria that can be used to create tests to ensure the software is developed correctly.

Agile teams vary in terms of how they document user stories. Regardless of the approach taken to document user stories, documentation should be concise and enough.

Non-functional requirements, such as usability and performance, are also important and can be specified as unique user stories or part of other functional user stories.

In the Agile project, User stories are the main test basis for creating test cases, but other possible test bases which can help the testers include:

- Detailed design
- Existing functions, features, and quality characteristics of the system
- Information on defects from existing and previous projects
- User profiles
- Quality risks
- Experience of tester from previous projects

Note

Tester's role in user story creation

- Help the team in creating and analyzing user stories
- Detect missing details by asking open-ended questions to the Product Owner and BA
- Identify missing functional and non-functional requirements in stories and help the team to complete them
- Confirming the acceptance criteria with the team

Summary:

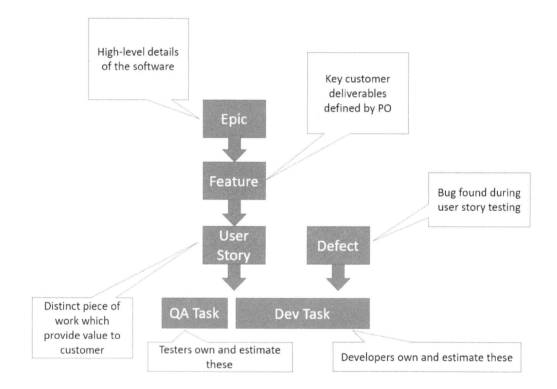

6 Difference between Traditional and Agile testing

In sequential development, testers are involved from the start of the project, but the major part of testing is still left until the end when the entire solution is fully developed. A frequent problem associated with this approach is that when the earlier stages overrun, particularly coding, the testing time is reduced. As testers get less time to finish the testing, it compromises the earlier agreed testing coverage and quality.

To overcome these issues, Agile development, complete the specification, design, build and test process in short iterations where each iteration results in working software that delivers features of value to business stakeholders. The development, integration, and testing activities take place throughout each iteration, these activities run in parallel and often overlap each other. Thus, testing activities occur throughout the iteration rather than a final activity.

Testers, developers, and business stakeholders all have a role in testing in Agile projects. Developers perform unit tests as they develop features from the user stories, and then the testers test those features. Business stakeholders also test the stories before implementation. They may use written test cases but are also likely to explore and experiment with features to provide fast feedback to the development team.

Note
Agile vs. traditional lifecycles

- Short iterations

- Each iteration provides software that has a "business value"

- After the iteration planning, the chosen user stories are developed, integrated, and tested

- Development, integration and test activities run in parallel

- As tasks overlap, iterations are very dynamic

Agile Test Levels

Test levels are test activities that are logically related based on the product's completeness or maturity under test.

In sequential lifecycle models, the test levels are often defined such that the exit criteria of one level are part of the entry criteria for the next level. Thus, the requirements must be validated and verified during requirement analysis before the solution design begins. Similarly, coded functions must be unit tested before integration testing can take place.

In Agile development, the test levels overlap. Thus, requirement specification, design specification, and development activities will overlap with test levels. This happens because changes to requirements, design, and code can happen at any point in an iteration.

During iteration, a user story will typically follow the test sequence:

- **Unit testing**- typically done by the developer(s)

- **Story testing**- which is sometimes split into two activities:

  - **Story verification testing**- involves testing against the user story's acceptance criteria. These tests are often automated and mostly performed by developers or testers.

  - **Story validation testing**- involves testing to confirm whether the feature is fit for use. These tests are often manually and tested by testers in collaboration with business stakeholders. This improves the visibility of the progress and gains real feedback from the business stakeholders.

Regression testing occurs throughout the iteration and frequently runs in parallel with automated unit tests and feature verification tests from the current iteration and previous iterations. Automated regression tests are mostly part of the continuous integration framework. Chapter 11 provides more details on continuous integration.

Some Agile projects have a system test level that starts as soon as the first user story is ready for testing. This involves executing functional tests and non-functional tests (performance, reliability, usability, and other test types).

Agile teams can employ various forms of acceptance testing, including user, operational, regulatory, and contract acceptance tests. For commercial off-the-shelf (COTS) software development, internal alpha tests (factory acceptance) and external beta tests (customer site) may also be applicable.

One of the objectives of acceptance testing is building confidence among potential or existing customers of the system.

Acceptance testing is performed at agreed, appropriate points in the development process. This happens likely at the end of each iteration, after completing each iteration, or after a series of iterations.

Exploratory testing

It is widely used in Agile projects due to the **limited time available for test analysis** and also due to the **limited details in the user stories**.

In exploratory testing, test cases are not pre-defined, but design, execution, test logging, and learning are carried out dynamically during test execution.

In this testing tester dynamically adjusts test goals during execution and prepares only lightweight documentation. The test results help learn more about the system and create tests for the areas that may require more testing.

This testing is guided by a prepared test charter. **A test charter** provides the test conditions to cover during a time-boxed testing session. During exploratory testing, the results of the most recent tests guide the next test.

A test charter may include the following information:

- **Actor**: The system user
- **Purpose**: Includes the objective that the actor wants to achieve (test conditions)
- **Setup**: What needs to be in place to start the test execution
- **Priority**: Relative importance of this charter, based on the priority of the associated user story or the risk level
- **Reference**: Specifications (e.g., user story), risks, or other information sources
- **Data**: Required to carry out the charter
- **Activities**: a list of possible scenarios that the actor may engage in and possible tests (positive and negative)
- **Oracle notes**: How to evaluate the product to determine correct results (e.g., to capture what happens on the screen and compare to what is written in the user's manual)
- **Variations**: Alternative actions and evaluations to complement the ideas described under activities

Before starting the testing, the testers should ask **relevant questions about what to test** to the business or system SME's. These will be contextually dependent but can include the following:

- What is most important to find out about the system?
- In what way may the system fail?

- What happens if......?
- What should happen when......?
- Are customer needs, requirements, and expectations fulfilled?

A **set of heuristics can be applied when testing**. A heuristic offers a set of guiding "rules of thumb" for testing and evaluating the results. Examples include:

- **CRUD**: Create, Read, Update, Delete e.g. create new entries, read/update/delete existing entries
- **Follow the Data**: Actions that enter, search, report, export, import, etc.
- **Configuration variations**: Change configuration data
- **Constraints**: Violate them. Leave mandatory fields null, etc.
- **Interruptions**: Log off, shut down, or reboot, disconnect, etc.
- **Multi-user**: CRUD from multiple logins

Agile encourages lightweight documentation, but it is important to record the test flow, so the testing activity is visible to other stakeholders. The following list provides examples of information that may be useful to document:

- **Test coverage**: Data used, how much has been covered, and how much is remaining.
- **Evaluation notes**: Observations during testing, do the system and feature under test seem to be stable, were any defects found, what is planned as the next step according to the current observations, and any other list of ideas.
- **Risk list**: Risks covered and remaining.
- **Issues, questions, and deviations**: Unexpected behavior, questions regarding the efficiency of the approach, concerns about the test environment, test data, test script, or the system under test
- **Actual behavior**: Recording of the actual behavior of the system that needs to be saved (e.g., video, screen captures, output data files)

To manage exploratory testing, a method called **session-based test management** can be used. A session is defined as an uninterrupted period of testing which could last from 60 to 120 minutes. Test sessions include the following:

- Survey session (to learn how it works)
- Analysis session (evaluation of the functionality or characteristics)
- Deep coverage (corner cases, scenarios, interactions)

Note

Test levels:

- **Sequential lifecycle models**- the exit criteria of one level are often part of the entry criteria of the next level

- **Iterative models** -test levels overlap with other test levels or with requirements, design and development activities

Agile Test levels:

- **Unit testing**: Typically done by a developer

- **Story testing** is split into

  - **Verification testing**: Often automate; testing against the user stories acceptance criteria by developer or tester

  - **Validation testing**: Manual; developer, tester and business stakeholders work together to check if it is fit for use

Exploratory testing

- Exploratory testing is widely used in Agile projects due to limited time for testing and limited information in user stories

- In exploratory testing test design and test execution occurs at the same time

- Test charters are used to guide exploratory testing and test session are used for uninterrupted testing in defined timeframes

Regression testing

- Occurs throughout the iteration

- Runs in parallel with automated unit tests and feature verification tests

Acceptance tests

- Takes places at close or after the completion of each iteration or after a series of iterations

- Can include user, operational, regulatory, and contract acceptance tests

- Alpha and beta tests can also be done based on the product

7 | Agile Team ceremonies

"Ceremonies" or meetings are an important part of Agile development. All the Agile team members attend and participate in these ceremonies. They bring a common goal and vision and share timely information and progress with all members.

Let's look at each of the agile ceremonies and understand how they empower the team and drive agile development.

Iteration planning (Sprint planning in Scrum)

Attendees Required: All team members working on iteration tasks

When: At the beginning of an iteration.

Duration: Usually an hour to a two-hour planning meeting. Sometimes a follow-up planning meeting is planned if the first one is not sufficient to discuss/estimate all the stories.

Purpose: Iteration planning is for the team to review, understand, agree, and estimate user stories included in the current sprint. The team picks the stories from the product backlog into the sprint backlog based on the priority of the stories and team velocity. (we will discuss velocity in later chapters) This meeting starts with the Product Owner providing the walk-through of selected stories and sprint objectives. In the process of user stories review, the team should ask the Product Owner necessary questions and ensure that they are clear with the story's business value. Once the user stories are clear to the team, the acceptance criteria are defined. Finally, the team estimates the stories using a poker planning session. (we will cover poker planning later in **chapter 10**)

Iteration Planning

- A team meeting to agree on the scope of iteration

- Extend the user stories to include acceptance criteria

- Clarification and estimation of user stories

Role of the tester

- During iteration planning, testers participated in team discussion to analyze and understand the stories

- They ask open-ended questions and examples to the Product Owner to clarify the stories

- They check that the acceptance criteria of the story are testable

- Verify that all the functional and non-functional attributes are included in the user story

- Testers also actively participate with other team members in the estimation of user stories

Daily stand-up (**Daily Scrum** in Scrum)

Attendees Required: All team members

Optional: Team Stakeholders

When: Once per day

Duration: 10- 15 minutes.

Purpose: This is a quick status meeting, the agenda for each member is:

- Work completed since the last meeting.
- Work planned for completion by the next meeting.
- Anything that is blocking the progress? (Impediments)

Iteration Review/Showcase (Sprint Review in Scrum)

Attendees Required: All team members, representatives from different customer groups (Product owners)

Optional: Project Stakeholders

When: Towards the end of the iteration

Duration: 30-60 minutes.

Purpose: Iteration review/showcase is used to demonstrate the work completed within the iteration to the Product Owner, business representatives, and other stakeholders. During this meeting the Product Owner or other participants ask for different scenarios to be demonstrated to get confidence about the functionality developed. The iteration review provides a way to gather immediate, contextual feedback from the stakeholders and different customer groups.

Note

Iteration Review/Showcase

- A team meeting to demonstrate the working software completed as part of iteration to the business

- The iteration review aims to get feedback from the stakeholders on the user stories worked during the iteration

Role of the tester

- Testers, as part of the team, actively participate with other team members in this ceremony

- Testers help the team running different scenarios during this session

- Testers can also help the team in verifying the environment and preparing test data before the showcase

---

Retrospective/Lessons Learnt (**Sprint Retrospective** in Scrum)

Attendees Required: All team members

When: At the end of an iteration.

Duration: 30-60 minutes.

Purpose: The retrospective is a meeting held by the Agile team to look back at an iteration (or a certain number of iterations) and discuss **what was successful**, **what could be improved**, and **how to incorporate the improvements and retain the successes** in the future iterations. Regularly conducted retrospective meetings are critical to self-organization and continual improvement of development and testing activities. Successful retrospective requires an atmosphere of mutual trust and respect, with a focus on improvement. The discussion in retrospectives is focused on the process rather than targeting any team member.

Note
Retrospective
• A team meeting at the end of each iteration to discuss
• What was successful,
• What can be improved
• How to retain successful habits and practices
• Focus is given to the process, practices, and tools
• The goal is continuous improvement and to incorporate improvements in future iterations
• A basic precondition for this meeting is a professional environment & trust among members of the team
Role of the tester
• Testers, as part of the team, play an important part in the retrospective
• Testers bring in their unique perspective to make a substantial contribution to the success of retrospective
• Discuss process improvement for both testing and non-testing activities
• Testers highlight bottlenecks and all their impediments faced in the sprint and suggest improvements to overcome these for future sprints.

Sprint Planning Meeting

Daily Scrum Meeting

Scrum Review Meeting

Scrum Retrospective Meeting

Ceremonies in Scrum

8 | Status reporting

Like traditional projects, in Agile projects, the team and stakeholders are interested to know the project's progress at regular intervals. In Agile projects, one of the measures of progress is by having working software at the end of each iteration. To determine when the team will have working software, all work items' progress need to be monitored during the iteration. Team members in Agile teams, including testers, utilize the following methods to communicate progress and status to the rest of the team and other stakeholders:

- Verbally during the stand-up meetings
- Using Agile Task Boards
- Using Burndown charts
- Using dashboards

Stand-up

Ad-hoc status updates happen due to co-location and collaboration, which are common in Agile projects. Also, formally scheduled daily stand-up meetings ensure that everyone is up to date about status.

The daily stand-up meeting includes all members of the Agile team, including testers. At this meeting, they communicate their current status to other team members. The agenda for each member is to provide the status of:

- Work completed since the last meeting.
- Work planned for completion by the next meeting.
- Anything that is blocking the progress?

Daily Stand-up Agenda

As issues that block test progress are communicated during the daily stand-up meetings, the whole team becomes aware of them and can help the testers in resolving them.

Agile Task Boards

Agile task boards provide an instant, detailed visual representation of the whole team's current status, including the status of testing. The story cards, development tasks, test tasks, and other tasks created during iteration planning are captured on the task board, often using different color cards to easily distinguish the task type.

During the iteration, progress is managed via the movement of these tasks across the task board into columns such as **To do, Development, Testing, UAT Testing and Done**. Testing tasks on the task board relate to the acceptance criteria defined for the user stories. As test automation scripts, manual tests, and exploratory tests for a test task achieve a passing status, the task moves into the **task board's UAT Testing** column. The status of tasks on the board is regularly reviewed by the team, both ad-hoc and during the daily stand-up meetings. This ensures tasks are moving across the board at an acceptable rate.

Backlog	To Do	Development	Testing	UAT	Done
User Stories	User Stories	User Stories	User Story		
		User Stories		User Story	
				User Story	
Defects	Defects				User Stories
					Defect
Tasks	Tasks	User Stories	Defect		

Task board

Burndown Charts

A burndown chart is a graphical representation of outstanding work versus time. The outstanding work is often on the vertical axis, with time along the horizontal. It is useful for predicting when all of the outstanding work will be completed.

Burndown charts are a common way to track progress within each iteration and across the entire release. These charts are simple to maintain, easy to read, and show the current state-of-play clearly.

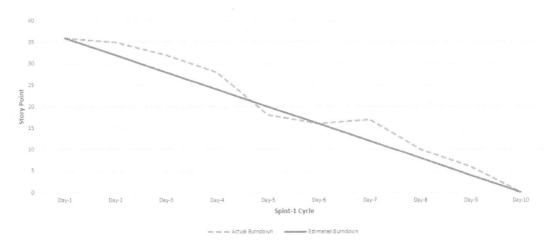

Iteration Burndown Chart

Dashboards

Agile teams often use software applications, e.g., JIRA, to maintain their story cards and Agile task boards. This method of communication also gathers metrics from the testing process. Communicating test status in such an automated manner also frees testers time to focus on designing and executing more tests.

Agile teams may use tools that automatically generate status reports based on test results and task progress, updating wiki dashboards and sending dashboard-style emails to the team.

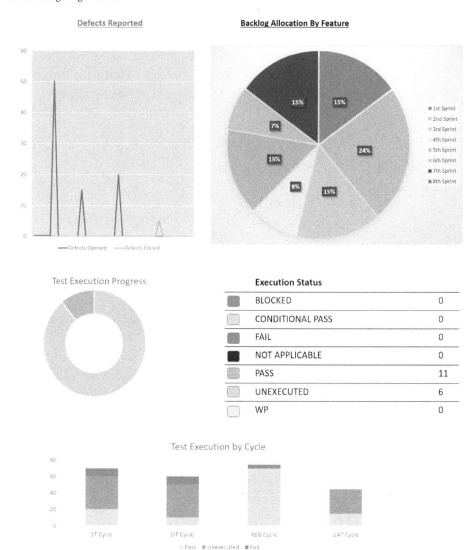

Typical wiki dashboards

Note
Ways to communicate test progress: • **Stand-up meetings** (verbal communication)- Team members communicate their current status, possible problems, and solutions • **Agile Task Boards** - An instant, detailed visualization of the team's current status, including test status • **Burndown chart**- A visual chart tracking the progress of the product during the project iterations or releases • **Dashboards**- wiki-style dashboards with the capability to automatically update the status report and send dashboard-style emails to all team members and interested parties

9 | Release and Iteration planning

In traditional projects, all the planning activities are done upfront; therefore, the team spends a significant amount of time on these activities at the start of the project. This approach is not very practical and helpful as the project team has limited information and limited knowledge of the software to be developed during the start of the project. Therefore, in order to make planning more effective, Agile projects divide the planning activities at release and iteration levels.

Release Planning

Release planning is concerned with the release of the product after the end of the number of iterations or a period of time. One of the main activities during release planning is to define the product backlog. Release plans are high-level as it happens well ahead of the start of a project.

In release planning, business representatives collaborate with the team to refine epic and features into a collection of smaller stories and then prioritize them for the release.

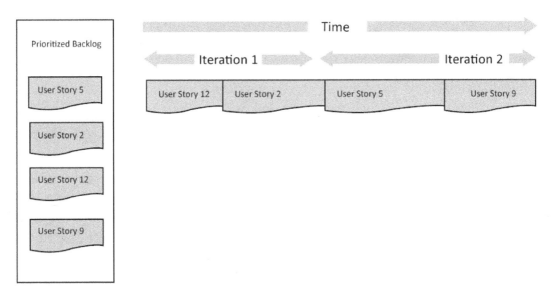

Release Planning

Based on these user stories, the team will identify project and product risks (quality risks) and do a high-level effort estimation. The testers can then formulate the test approach and test plan for the release spanning all the iterations based on these identified risks.

Testers are involved in release planning and especially add value in the following activities:

- Defining testable user stories
- Contributing to project and quality risk analysis
- High-level estimation of user stories
- Defining the necessary test levels
- Planning all the testing activities required for the release

Note
Following activities happen during Release planning:

- User stories for the release are defined and prioritized
- Product Backlog is created
- Estimation of effort is performed at a high-level
- Test Strategy and Test plan are defined based on the identified project and product risk

Iteration Planning

Iteration planning is done as a first thing after the start of each iteration. Iteration planning looks ahead only until the end of a single iteration and is concerned with preparation of the iteration backlog.

In iteration planning, the team selects high-priority user stories from the release backlog. These stories are then elaborated, and risk analysis is performed on these user stories. The team then conducts an estimation of these stories and then creates tasks required to complete the story.

During the iteration planning meeting, in order to understand the user story, the team may ask clarifying questions to the business representatives and they must provide answers so the team can understand how to develop and test each story. Once the team is clear about the story and has all the information, they can start defining the acceptance criteria.

If a user story is ambiguous and attempts to clarify with business representatives fail, the team can move it back to the backlog and select the next high-priority story from the backlog.

The number of stories selected is based on established team velocity and the sum of the selected user stories' estimated size. For example, if the established team velocity is 20 story points, then the team can pick four user stories worth five story points each (based on the highest business priority). If there is no exact match, the sum of story points can be taken to the nearest velocity. Calculation of velocity is discussed in detail in chapter 16. Once the iteration contents are finalized, the user stories are broken into tasks, which the appropriate team members carry out.

Release Backlog	Iterations Backlog	To Do	Development	Testing	Completed (Done)
User Stories	User Stories	User Story	User Story	User Story	
		User Story			
		Defect	Tasks	User Story	User Story
		User Story			

Iteration Planning

Testers are involved in iteration planning and especially add value in the following activities:

- Participating in the detailed risk analysis of user stories
- Determining the testability of the user stories
- Identifying functional and non-functional aspects to be tested
- Creating story acceptance tests
- Creating tasks (particularly testing tasks) for the user stories
- Estimation of stories
- Supporting and participating in test automation at multiple levels of testing

---

Note

Following activities happen during iteration planning:

- The team selects user stories from the prioritized release backlog

- Selected user stories are then elaborated

- Risk analysis is performed on these selected stories

- Estimation is done for the work-related to each user story

- The team collaborate to understand what is necessary to implement and test each story

- The business representatives help the team to understand the story by providing answers to team questions

- If attempts to clarify a vague user story fail, the team can '**push**' the story back to the backlog and '**pull**' the next high priority story

- After the contents of the iteration are agreed upon, user stories are broken into tasks which the appropriate team members carry out

- Velocity (story points per iteration) indicates the productivity of the team and limits the selections of user stories for a particular iteration

---

Changes are inevitable in Agile projects. Internal or external factors may trigger these changes. Internal factors may arise due to delivery capabilities, technical issues, or budget constraints. External factors can be due to the discovery of new markets and opportunities, new competitors, or business threats. These factors can change the release plans and may affect the release objectives and/or target dates.

The same applies to iteration plans which may change during iteration. For example, a particular user story that was considered relatively simple during estimation might prove more complex than expected.

Such changes can be challenging for testers. Testers must understand the "big picture" of the release for test planning purposes and make sure that they have all the information about the changes before starting their testing activities. While the required information must be available to the tester early, changes must also be embraced as demanded by Agile principles. This is a dilemma that requires careful decisions about test strategies and test documentation.

Release and iteration planning should address test planning as well as development planning. Particular test-related issues to address include:

- The scope of testing, the extent of testing for those areas in scope, the test goals, and the rationale for these decisions.
- The team members who will carry out the test activities.
- The test environment and test data requirement
- The timing, sequencing, dependencies (including how the test activities relate to and depend on development activities), and prerequisites for the functional and non-functional test activities. Examples include how frequently to run regression tests; which stories are dependent on other stories or any other test data dependencies.
- The project and quality risks to be addressed
- The team estimation efforts for user stories include the time and effort needed to complete the required testing activities.

Note
• Release planning is concerned with the planning for the release of the entire product whereas, iteration planning is concerned with the planning for the current iteration.   • Changes can affect both the release and iteration planning.

10 Estimation

The Agile team estimates the effort required to complete a particular user story, including analysis, development, and testing effort. It is done at a high-level during the release planning and detailed during the iteration planning.

The most common estimation technique used in Agile projects is **planning poker,** which is a consensus-based technique based on relative estimating. The values used for estimation can be a Fibonacci sequence or any other choice progression (e.g., shirt sizes ranging from extra-small to extra-large). The values represent the number of story points, effort days, or other units in which the team estimates.

The Fibonacci sequence (i.e., 0, 1, 2, 3, 5, 8, 13, 21, …) is recommended for the deck cards because the numbers in the sequence reflect that uncertainty grows proportionally with the size of the story. A high estimate usually means that the story is not well understood or should be broken down into multiple smaller stories.

Following are the sequence of activities for a planning poker session:

1. Product Owner or customer representative explains the purpose of the user story and the business value it presents

2. The team discusses the user story for any clarifications.

3. Once the story is clear team starts the estimation, each team member privately selects one card from the deck of cards to represent their estimated story points (generally, a reference story is used, and the team member compares the story with reference to arrive at a story point.)

4. The cards are revealed, and values are being compared.

5. If all the estimates are of the same value, it is considered final.

6. For unequal estimation values, a discussion is started; usually, the team member with the highest and the lowest value will provide their reasoning.

7. Then another round is 'played' until an agreement is reached either by consensus or by applying rules (e.g., use the median, average, or use the highest score) to limit the number of poker rounds.

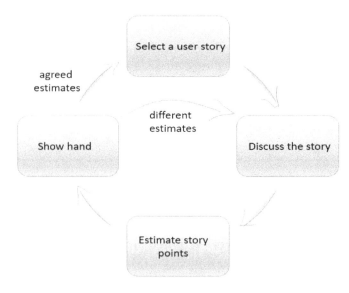

Planning Poker

We will see how the poker planning is done in the real projects in chapter 16.

Note
• Planning poker is a consensus-based technique for estimation
• The team assesses the story point based on the relative size of each task associated with the story
• Aspects such as development and testing effort, the complexity of the story, risk level, and testing scope play a key role in the estimation.
• Assessment/evaluation of the effort can be done using story points by means of planning poker cards using Fibonacci numbers or T-shirt sizes: (**S**)mall, (**M**)edium, (**L**)arge, and (**xL**) extra large
• Discussion of the story during poker planning helps the team gets a common understanding of the features
• A higher estimate means the story is too complex and should be split up into smaller stories if possible.

11 **Automation**

One of the core Agile principle is that requirement changes can occur throughout the project. Changing the existing features have testing implications, particularly around regression testing. Automated testing is one way of managing the amount of test effort associated with these changes. With the emphasis on test automation in Agile projects, manual testing is likely to focus more on exploratory testing.

As there is a lot of emphasis on test automation at all levels in Agile-based projects, testers in Agile projects spend considerable time creating, executing, monitoring and maintaining automated scripts. Developers focus on creating automated unit tests, whereas testers focus on creating automated integration, system, and system integration tests. This is one of the reasons that the testers in Agile teams should have some technical and test automation background.

Test automation pyramid

In Agile projects, the test pyramid is often used to illustrate three different layers of automated tests. The bottom layer represents the automated unit or component tests and supports all the other tests. In Agile development, the aim is to push as many tests as possible to this layer.

The middle layer represents most of the API tests which run behind the presentation layer and cover a more extensive set of functionalities directly without going through the GUI.

The top layer represents the test cases that are done through the GUI and test the presentation layer. These tests are written once all the coding is completed. The Agile team tries to minimize the number of tests at this layer. There are few manual tests on the top of the pyramid, which shows that there will always be tests that will be run manually, i.e., exploratory tests and UAT tests.

The team should have the automation test strategy based on the concept of the test pyramid. Testers can share this concept with other stakeholders to emphasize more automation for tests on the lower levels.

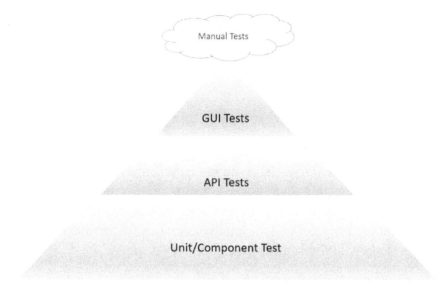

Test Automation Pyramid

Note
• The pyramid represents a larger number of automated tests at the lower test levels (bottom of the pyramid) and a smaller number of tests at the upper test levels (top of the pyramid)
• Test automation pyramid can be used to plan the automation strategy for Agile teams

Testing quadrants

Brian Marick defi ned the Agile Testing Quadrants to clarify the link between test levels and appropriate test types. Each of the four quadrants refl ects the reason we do testing.

The testing quadrants model and its variants help ensure that all-important test types and test levels are included in the development lifecycle. This model also provides a way to differentiate and describe the types of tests to all stakeholders, including developers, testers, and business representatives.

The **X-axis** shows the tests that **support the team** and **critiques the product**; on the other hand, **and Y-axis** shows the tests that are **business-facing** and **technology-facing**. Quadrant numbers are for identifi cation only, and the order in which they are numbered does not imply the sequence of testing.

In the testing quadrants, tests can be business (user) or technology (developer) facing. Some tests support the work done by the Agile team and confirm software behavior while other tests are used to verify the product. Tests can be fully manual, fully automated, a combination of manual and automated, or manual but supported by tools.

The four quadrants are as follows:

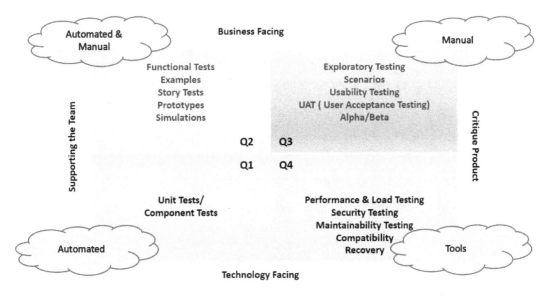

Agile Testing Quadrants

- **Quadrant Q1** is **unit level**, technology facing, and supports the developers. It contains **unit and component tests**. Unit tests are used to analyze and define software behavior and are written before the code is produced. Q1 tests should be automated and included in the continuous integration process.

- **Quadrant Q2** is **system-level**, business-facing, and confirms product behavior. This quadrant contains **functional tests, examples, story tests, user experience prototypes, and simulations**. These tests check the acceptance criteria and can be manual or automated. They are often created during the user story development and thus improve the quality of the stories. They are useful when creating automated regression test suites. Q2 includes both manual and/or automated test types.

- **Quadrant Q3** is **system or user acceptance level**, business-facing, and contains tests that critique the product, using realistic scenarios and data. This quadrant contains **exploratory testing, scenarios, process flows, usability testing, user acceptance testing, alpha testing, and beta testing**. These tests are often manual and are user-oriented.

- **Quadrant Q4** is **technology-facing and** contains tests that critique the product. It is the system or operational acceptance level and contains **performance, load, stress, scalability, security, maintainability, memory management, compatibility, interoperability, data migration, infrastructure, and recovery testing**. Tools are required to run most of these tests.

During any given iteration, tests from any or all quadrants may be required. The testing quadrants apply to **dynamic testing** rather than static testing.

Note
• Testing quadrants align the test levels with the appropriate test types
• The use of this model ensures that all-important test types and test levels are included in the development lifecycle
• Helps to describe and differentiate types of tests to all stakeholders, including developers, testers, and business representatives
• During any given iteration, tests from one, several, or all quadrants may be required
• The testing quadrants are only applicable to dynamic testing

Continuous Integration tools

In Agile projects, as the development and testing activities run in parallel, continuous integration tools are required so multiple developers can make changes to the shared code repository and integrate all the changed components regularly. Continuous integration tools merge all changes made to the software and periodically integrate all modified components at least once a day. Configuration management, compilation, software build, deployment, and testing are wrapped into a single, automated, repeatable process. Since developers integrate their work constantly, it helps in earlier detection of integration problems and conflicting changes. It provides frequent feedback to the development team on whether the code is working.

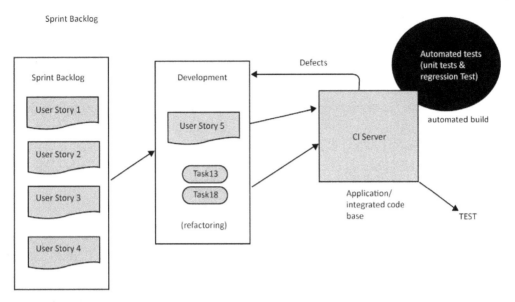

Continuous Integration Process

Once the developers code, debug, and check-in of code into a shared source code repository, a continuous integration process consisting of the following automated activities are triggered:

- **Static code analysis**: The CI server performs static code analysis and reports results.

- **Compile**: The code is compiled and linked to generate executables files.

- **Unit test**: The CI server executes unit tests, check code coverage and report results.

- **Deploy**: The software build is deployed into a test environment.

- **Integration test**: Integration tests are executed, and the results are reported.

- **Report**: The results of the activities above are posted at a well visible location(dashboard) and/or are sent as a status email to the team.

An automated build and test process take place on a daily basis and detects integration errors early and quickly. Continuous integration allows Agile testers to run automated tests as part of the continuous integration process and get quick feedback on the quality of the code. These test results are visible to all team members when automated reports are integrated into the process. Good automated regression tests cover as much functionality as possible, including user stories delivered in the previous iterations. Good coverage in automated regression tests helps support building and testing large integrated systems. When the regression testing is automated, the Agile testers are freed to focus on the current iteration testing activities.

In addition to running unit and integration tests, CI tools can run additional static and dynamic tests, measure and profile performance, extract and format documentation from the source code, and facilitate manual quality assurance processes. This can result in a significant reduction of time taken to implement continuous quality control.

Build tools linked to automatic deployment tools can fetch the appropriate build from the continuous integration or build server and deploy it into different environments for testing or other purposes. This reduces the errors to install releases in different environments. It also reduces dependencies on team members who are specialized in these tasks, and the whole process is more streamlined and quicker.

Note
Benefits of properly implemented CI tool • Earlier detection and easier root cause analysis of integration problems and conflicting changes • Frequent feedback is provided to the development team on whether the code is working • Provides confidence on a solid foundation for every day's work and reduces regression risks • Makes progress toward the completion of a product increment visible to developers and testers • Eliminates the risks associated with scheduling a big-bang integration • An executable software is constantly available throughout the sprint for testing or demonstration purposes • Reduction of repetitive manual testing activities, so testers get more time to run the exploratory test • Quick feedback on decisions made for quality improvement and testing

12 Quality Risks

Like traditional projects, Agile projects also use a risk-based approach to prioritize the tasks and user stories based on the level of quality risk associated with them. Tasks and user stories associated with higher risks should start earlier and involve more rigorous testing and more effort. Tasks and user stories related to lower risks should start later and may involve less testing effort. This also helps the testers in the proper selection, allocation, and prioritization of test conditions.

Testers commonly use risk identification, analysis, and risk mitigation strategies to make a judgment on

- The extent of testing to be carried out
- Prioritization of testing
- Test techniques to be employed
- Selecting the appropriate number of test cases for execution

Quality Risk Analysis

The quality risk analysis process performed in the Agile project is outlined in the following steps:

1. **Identify quality risks**

    a. The whole Agile team meets to identify the risks.

    b. All backlog items are displayed.

    c. The team discusses each item's quality characteristics and agrees on any quality risk that may emerge.

2. **Analyze each risk**

    a. The team categorizes the risk. Example categories include product, project, business, and technical risks.

b. The team assesses the likelihood of the failure based on functional and technical complexity and relates to the potential/expected impact to the business if the function does not work as expected.

c. Based on the combined Business Criticality and Likelihood of failure, Test Prioritization Matrix is prepared. Each User story is then assigned one of the following three values from the matrix.

		Likelihood of Failure		
		3 - Low	2 - Medium	1 - High
Business Criticality	A - High	P1	P1	P1
	B - Medium	P2	P2	P1
	C – Low	P3	P3	P2

Key
P1 – Priority 1
P2 – Priority 2
P3 – Priority 3

Test Prioritization Matrix

3. **Define tests**

a. The team selects appropriate test techniques to mitigate the risk based on the level of risk and the relevant quality characteristics (functionality, reliability, usability, etc.).

b. The team determines the extent of testing required given the level of risk.

Quality Risk Analysis

In Agile projects, **quality risk analysis** takes place during both release and iteration planning.

- **During Release planning**: The business representative(s) may provide an overview of the features that will be included in the release and any perceived risks associated with them. The Agile team with the help of relevant stakeholders, will contribute to the discussions and help to identify and validate the risk and assess further ones. Based on this the team will assign a risk rating to all the stories which are part of the product backlog.

- **During Iteration planning**: The team will pick the stories from the product backlog based on the associated risk and business priority. Once the user stories are agreed for the iteration the team will assess them for risks. The stories with greater risk may be started first as more testing will be required for high-risk items and fewer for the low-priority risk items. Risk-based testing has the advantage that the most critical areas of the system are tested first. This will minimize the risk even if there are any delays or problems that result in testing being curtailed.

Note
In Agile projects, new changes may have an impact on the quality risks identified earlier. Therefore, quality risk analysis should be revisited periodically, especially when new changes are introduced to the project. Adjustments may be required where new risks have emerged, the level of existing risks change, and the effectiveness of existing risk mitigation activities may require examination and remediation.

13 Tools used by Agile teams

To support the testing activities or increase the efficiency and accuracy of testing, the testing team often uses tools. These testing tools can be used to support one or more testing activities. Some tools are directly used in testing, such as test execution and test data preparation. In contrast, other tools support the testing activities, such as content creation, reporting, and collaboration with other team members. Following is the list of the most common tools used in Agile project:

Content creation and collaboration tools (e.g. Atlassian Confluence)

These tools allow teams to build and share an **online knowledge base with the content and knowledge** on various aspects of the project, including the following:

- **Product feature diagrams, feature discussions requirements documents, release notes, roadmaps, prototype diagrams**, **Agile boards**, which can be used in team meetings and workshops.

- **Development/testing tools and techniques** information which can be easily shared with other team members.

- **Metrics, charts, and dashboards** related to product status (if the tool is integrated with the build and task management tool, the status is automatically updated).

- **Conversations between team members** which can be helpful for other team members, e.g. discussion regarding the feature between the developers and Product Owner, meeting notes.

Confluence is a widely used tool for content creation and collaboration in Agile projects. It connects teams with the content, knowledge, and coworkers they need to get work done faster. Confluence spaces are great for creating and organizing rich content for meeting notes, project plans, requirements documents, release notes, roadmaps, and more.

Test case management tools (e.g. JIRA, ALM)

These tools are used by the testers and other team members of the Agile team to **manage the test cases** for different phases. These tools may be part of the whole team's application lifecycle management or task management tool. These tools can be used to manage the test case other than providing visibility into the current state of the application, especially with distributed teams.

Exploratory test tools (e.g. XRAY, TestBench)

Exploratory testing is done without any formal test cases, so it is difficult to replicate the steps if any defects are found. These tools **record the activity performed during exploratory test** sessions. As they record the actions taken it can be useful when a defect is found, as the recording can be used by the testers to replicate the defects and provide details in the defect report.

Continuous integration tools (e.g. Jenkins, TeamCity)

These tools help multiple developers to make changes to the shared code repository and integrate all the changed components regularly. This makes it easier for users to obtain a fresh build. Characteristics of these tools include:

- Allows regular code changes into a shared code repository
- Earlier detection of integration problems and conflicting changes
- Provides frequent feedback to the development team on whether the code is working
- Improved collaboration within the team
- Reduced risk of code regression
- Version control within the various patch and product releases
- The capability of roll-back if there are some issues with the current build version

Test Automation Tool (e.g., Selenium, Cucumber)

These tools enable tests to be executed automatically or semi-automatically, using stored inputs and expected outcomes, through the use of a scripting language. These tools have ability to manipulate the tests with limited effort. For example, to repeat the test with different data or to test a different part of the system with similar steps and providing a test log for each test run.

Cucumber

Cucumber is open source, and hence it is free to use, and the feature files, readable for everyone in the team. This tool is based on Behavior Driven Development (BDD) framework, which is used to write tests in Gherkin. It allows users such as Business Analysts, Developers, Testers, etc., to automate the functionality in an easily readable and understandable format which is one of the most outstanding features of this tool. The example of a feature file for testing the invalid username and password which can be tried with a set of test data (called as examples in script):

```
Scenario: User enter invalid username and password

Given the user navigate to homepage

When the user writes the username <username> and the
password <password>

And the user clicks on the login button

Then the user is still in the login page

Examples:
    |username|  |password|
    |abc|   |456|
    |xy@|   |def|
    |567|   |def|
```

BDD framework is beneficial when the need to turn the scenarios into automated tests rises. The scenarios already give the steps – the automation engineer simply needs to write a method/function to perform each step's operations.

For more information on Cucumber, check **https://cucumber.io/**

Selenium

Selenium is a free (open source) automated testing suite for web applications across different browsers and platforms. It focuses on automating web-based applications. It is very helpful in automating functional test cases. Selenium is not just a single tool but a suite of software, each one arranged for different testing needs of a project. It has four components:

- Selenium Integrated Development Environment (IDE)
- Selenium GRID

- Selenium Remote Control
- WebDriver

For more information on Selenium, check **https://www.selenium.dev/**

Selenium and Cucumber are a great combination for web application automation, as Cucumber allows you to write your tests quickly in English-like language. On the other hand, Selenium allows you to run on various combinations of browsers.

When using them together for test automation, tests are written in feature files that can be understood by various stakeholders in an agile environment. Cucumber also comes with its ability to support multiple scripts and programming languages, and JUnit is used to execute these scripts and generate the output.

14 | Applying Agile Testing in the context of Project

To understand how testing is carried out in an Agile project, we will consider testing for a fictitious bank named "Global Sun," which is not related to any real entity with the same or similar name.

The Global Sun bank is one of the growing consumer banks (retail banks) responsible for sales and service of around 1.2 million customers in Australia. To assist the customers with their everyday banking needs, activities are conducted through the Global Sun bank's nationwide network of branches, call centers, ATM terminals, and internet banking services. The Global Sun bank's typical product include **savings and transactional accounts**, **mortgages**, and **credit cards**.

Currently, the Global Sun customers must visit bank branches to do an international money transfer, which is a tedious and time-consuming activity. Most of the Global Sun competitors have online systems for international money transfer. Global Sun is planning to develop a new solution so that the customers can perform International Money Transfer (IMT) via the Global Sun Online banking site. The money will be transferred electronically from the Global Sun account to the overseas account within 2-3 business days. The customer should be able to send money to over 103 countries without visiting the branch by directly using this IMT system.

Once implemented, the IMT solution will provide the following benefits:

- **Fast Electronic Transfer**– The money is transferred electronically from the Global Sun account to the overseas account within 2-3 business days.

- **Real-time market rates-** While transferring via Global Sun internet banking, customers can see the real-time market rates for forex, and they can take advantage of exchange rate movements during the day and lock in the rate that suits them.

- **Staff independent service** – Customers can perform this entire transfer from their online banking site without any interaction with bank staff.

This system will reduce customer dependency on bank staff and increase the customer base, resulting in long-term cost benefits. The bank has decided to use Scrum for development for this project. As we have discussed earlier, Scrum is an agile framework for developing, delivering, and sustaining complex software products and is widely used for greenfield projects.

15 | Sprint Zero

Once the project is approved, the key members of the team can start working on preparation for sprint zero. It is the first iteration of the project mainly reserved for the majority of planning and preparation activities. This sprint is used for periods of planning and preparation for the entire release, the duration of this sprint is usually more than the normal sprint. Sprint zero sets the direction for what testing needs to achieve and how testing needs to achieve it throughout the sprints. The following tasks will be done as part of sprint zero for the IMT project:

1. Preparation of the product backlog

The Product Owner of IMT team with the help of business analyst and other team members will start defining the requirements so they can create the product backlog. This will require first defining the requirements in the form of EPIC → Features → User Stories

The Epic for the Online banking IMT project will be:

"Online solution for Global Sun Banking customers so they can perform International Money Transfer (IMT) via Global Sun Online banking site."

Now the team defines the Features which are considered in scope for this Epic. The main features selected for the Online banking IMT project are:

1. Entitlements (Access Control) for IMT eligible customers
2. Facilitate international money transfer
3. Error handling for transfer screens
4. Customer receives a transfer confirmation
5. Account Balances after the transfer

Now it is time to define which user stories are required under each feature to achieve the project goal. During Sprint Zero, high level user stories are identified which will be further refined during the sprints. Following are the high-level user stories created for IMT project.

1. **Entitlements (Access Control) for IMT eligible customers**
   a. **International transfer Menu item on the GS Banking System Screen**
      i. As an authorized GS online banking user for International transfers, I want to have a menu option, so that I can initiate an international transfer.

2. **Facilitate international transfer**
   a. **International Transfer (IMT) main screen**
      i. As a GS Online Banking user on IMT main screen, I want my eligible Accounts to be populated, so that I can select the account which can be used to initiate the transfer.
      ii. As a GS Online Banking user on the IMT main screen, I want the list of eligible countries to be populated, so that I can select the Beneficiary's bank location from the list.
      iii. As a GS Online Banking user on the IMT main screen, I want Beneficiary's account details fields, so that I can enter the Beneficiary's bank account number or IBAN for International transfer and Beneficiary's Bank SWIFT/BIC code for International transfer.
      iv. As a GS Online Banking user on the IMT main screen, I want an option under Beneficiary's bank details, so that I can enter the beneficiary's name for International transfer.
      v. As a GS Online Banking user on the IMT main screen, I want the eligible list of countries to be populated under the Beneficiary's details, so that I can select the beneficiary's country of location.
      vi. As a GS Online Banking user on the IMT main screen, I want an option under Beneficiary's details, so that I can enter the beneficiary's primary address for International transfer.
      vii. As a GS Online Banking user on the IMT main screen, I want an option under Beneficiary's details, so that I can enter the beneficiary's secondary address for International transfer.
      viii. As a GS Online Banking user on the IMT main screen, I want an option under Beneficiary's details, so that I can enter the message for the beneficiary for the International transfer.
      ix. As a GS Online Banking user on the IMT main screen, I want an option under Beneficiary's details to enter description of transfer, so that I can see the details in my statement.

 x. As a GS Online Banking user on the IMT main screen, I must fill all the mandatory fields, so that I can proceed to the international transfer detail screen.

b. International Transfer details screen

 i. As a GS Online Banking user on the IMT Transfer details screen, I want an option under Transfer details, so that I can enter the amount for the International transfer.

 ii. As a GS Online Banking user on the IMT Transfer details screen, I want to see the amount including any additional fees associated for my international transfer, so that I aware of the Total cost for the transfer.

 iii. As a GS Online Banking user on the IMT Transfer details screen, I want to have an option to pay the fees for international transfer from my account or from transferred funds, so that I can select appropriate option.

 iv. As a GS Online Banking user on the IMT Transfer details screen, I want to see the amount including any additional fees associated with my international transfer, so that I aware of the Total cost for the transfer.

 v. As a GS Online Banking user on the IMT Transfer details screen, I want to see the current exchange rate for international transfer with the retrieval time, so that I decide on my transfer based on the exchange rate

 vi. As a GS Online Banking user on the IMT Transfer details screen, I want to see the amount that the beneficiary will receive, so that I aware how much amount beneficiary will receive in their currency.

 vii. As a GS Online Banking user on the IMT Transfer details screen, I want to view the terms and conditions for my international transfer, so that I can acknowledge them.

 viii. As a GS Online Banking user on the IMT Transfer details screen, I want an option to go back to the International Transfer main screen, so that I can modify the previously entered details.

 ix. As a GS Online Banking user on the IMT Transfer details screen, I want to proceed to the next screen, so that I can confirm the details entered for the international transfer.

c. Transfer confirmation screen

 i. As a GS Online Banking user on the IMT Transfer confirmation screen, I want to see the Total amount that will be transferred, so that I confirm the amount before final transfer.

 ii. As a GS Online Banking user on the IMT Transfer confirmation screen, I want to see the selected debit account, so that I confirm the account details before final transfer.

 iii. As a GS Online Banking user on the IMT Transfer confirmation screen, I want to see the beneficiary account, so that I confirm the beneficiary account details before final transfer.

iv. As a GS Online Banking user on the IMT Transfer confirmation screen, I want to see the payment date & disclaimer, so that I am aware when the beneficiary will receive the payment.

v. As a GS Online Banking user on the IMT Confirmation screen, I want an option to go back to the International Transfer detail screen, so that I can modify the previously entered details.

vi. As a GS Online Banking user on the IMT Transfer Confirmation screen, I want to proceed to the next screen, so that I can confirm the details entered for the international transfer

d. Transfer Receipt screen

i. As a GS Online Banking user on the Transfer Receipt screen, I want to see the final transfer details, so that I can keep the receipt for my records.

ii. As a GS Online Banking user on the Transfer Receipt screen, I want to see a receipt number for my transfer, so that I can use it for tracking the transfer

iii. As a GS Online Banking user on the Transfer Receipt screen, I want to have an option to print the confirmation details., so that I keep a receipt of transfer for tracking and future reference

3. Error handling for transfer screens

a. International Transfer main screen

i. As a GS Online Banking user on the IMT main screen, I want to see an appropriate error message if the entered account number or IBAN is invalid, so that I can modify it before the transfer

ii. As a GS Online Banking user on the IMT main screen, I want to see an appropriate error message if the entered SWIFT code is invalid, so that I can modify it before the transfer

b. International Transfer details screen

i. As a GS Online Banking user on the IMT Transfer details screen, I want to see an appropriate error message if I have entered amount which is not in the range specified by the bank, so that I can modify the amount to be in range.

ii. As a GS Online Banking user on the IMT Transfer details screen, I want to see an appropriate error message if the total cost is greater than my account balance, so that I can change the transfer amount.

iii. As a GS Online Banking user on the IMT Transfer details screen, I want to see an appropriate error message if I have missed to enter any of the mandatory detail, so that I can enter them now.

iv. As a GS Online Banking user on the IMT Transfer details screen, I want to see an appropriate error message if I have not acknowledged the terms and conditions for the transfer, so that I read and acknowledge them.

4. Customer receives the Transfer confirmation

    i.   As a GS Online Banking user who has completed an international transfer, I want to receive the receipt of my transfer to my email, which I have provided to the bank, so that I can use that for tracking and future reference.

    ii. As a GS Online Banking user who has completed an international transfer, I want to receive the receipt of my transfer as a notification to my internet banking mailbox, so that I can use that for tracking and future reference.

5. Account Balances after the transfer

    i.   As a GS Online Banking user who has completed an international transfer, my account balance must be updated, so that I am aware of my current balance immediately after the transfer.

Note
Once the user stories are prepared, the Product Owner will assign priority to these user stories based on the importance to the business. Then the team will do the risk analysis exercise; based on that, they assign a risk rating to each story. A high-level estimation for each story follows this.

Priority of User story

Generally, in projects, the priority of stories is defined using the **MoSCoW** technique. The term MoSCoW itself is an acronym derived from the first letter of each of four prioritization categories: **M** - Must haves **S** - Should haves **C** - Could haves **W** - Won't haves

1: **Must-haves**- Must-have stories are critical in order for the project to be successful. The whole project may fail if one of the must-have stories is not implemented.

2: **Should-haves** – Should-have stories are important for the project to succeed but not as time-critical as Must-haves; the project will not fail if one of them is not implemented or implemented later. For example, a password reset can be a should-have user story for a project if a support team can reset the passwords manually during the first few months.

3: **Could-haves** - These stories may improve the overall customer experience, but they are not critical. They're usually related to improving error messages or adjusting how the application will look on certain devices.

4: **Won't-haves** - These stories have the lowest business value, and by not implementing them, there will be no significant impact on the project.

Risk rating of the User story

1: High-risk areas for business
2: Medium risk areas for business
3: Low-risk areas for business

By the end of Sprint Zero, the following product backlog is ready with an assigned priority and Risk rating for each story.

User Story #	Feature	User Story details	Priority	Risk Rating
IMT-01	Entitlements (Access Control) for IMT eligible customers	As an authorized GS online banking user for International transfers, I want to have a menu option, so that I can initiate an international transfer.	1	1
IMT-02	Facilitate international money transfer	As a GS Online Banking user on IMT main screen, I want my eligible Accounts to be populated, so that I can select the account which can be used to initiate the transfer.	1	2
IMT-03	Facilitate international money transfer	As a GS Online Banking user on the IMT main screen, I want the list of eligible countries to be populated, so that I can select the Beneficiary's bank location from the list.	1	1
IMT-04	Facilitate international money transfer	As a GS Online Banking user on the IMT main screen, I want Beneficiary's account details fields, so that I can enter the Beneficiary's bank account number or IBAN for International transfer and Beneficiary's Bank SWIFT/BIC code for International transfer.	1	1
IMT-05	Facilitate international money transfer	As a GS Online Banking user on the IMT main screen, I want an option under Beneficiary's bank details, so that I can enter the beneficiary's name for International transfer.	1	2
IMT-06	Facilitate international money transfer	As a GS Online Banking user on the IMT main screen, I want the eligible list of countries to be populated under the Beneficiary's details, so that I can select the beneficiary's country of location.	1	1
IMT-07	Facilitate international money transfer	As a GS Online Banking user on the IMT main screen, I want an option under Beneficiary's details, so that I can enter the beneficiary's primary address for International transfer.	2	3
IMT-08	Facilitate international money transfer	As a GS Online Banking user on the IMT main screen, I want an option under Beneficiary's details, so that I can enter the beneficiary's secondary address for International transfer.	3	3

User Story #	Feature	User Story details	Priority	Risk Rating
IMT-09	Facilitate international money transfer	As a GS Online Banking user on the IMT main screen, I want an option under Beneficiary's details, so that I can enter the message for the beneficiary for the International transfer.	3	3
IMT-10	Facilitate international money transfer	As a GS Online Banking user on the IMT main screen, I want an option under Beneficiary's details to enter description of transfer, so that I can see the details in my statement.	4	3
IMT-11	Facilitate international money transfer	As a GS Online Banking user on the IMT main screen, I must fill all the mandatory fields, so that I can proceed to the international transfer detail screen.	1	2
IMT-12	Facilitate international money transfer	As a GS Online Banking user on the IMT Transfer details screen, I want an option under Transfer details, so that I can enter the amount for the International transfer.	1	1
IMT-13	Facilitate international money transfer	As a GS Online Banking user on the IMT Transfer details screen, I want to see the amount including any additional fees associated for my international transfer, so that I aware of the Total cost for the transfer.	1	2
IMT-14	Facilitate international money transfer	As a GS Online Banking user on the IMT Transfer details screen, I want to have an option to pay the fees for international transfer from my account or from transferred funds, so that I can select appropriate option.	1	2
IMT-15	Facilitate international money transfer	As a GS Online Banking user on the IMT Transfer details screen, I want to see the amount including any additional fees associated with my international transfer, so that I aware of the Total cost for the transfer .	1	1
IMT-16	Facilitate international money transfer	As a GS Online Banking user on the IMT Transfer details screen, I want to see the current exchange rate for international transfer with the retrieval time, so that I decide on my transfer based on the exchange rate	1	1
IMT-17	Facilitate international money transfer	As a GS Online Banking user on the IMT Transfer details screen, I want to see the amount that the beneficiary will receive, so that I aware how much amount beneficiary will receive in their currency.	2	2
IMT-18	Facilitate international money transfer	As a GS Online Banking user on the IMT Transfer details screen, I want to view the terms and conditions for my international transfer, so that I can acknowledge them.	1	3

User Story #	Feature	User Story details	Priority	Risk Rating
IMT-19	Facilitate international money transfer	As a GS Online Banking user on the IMT Transfer details screen, I want an option to go back to the International Transfer main screen, so that I can modify the previously entered details.	3	3
IMT-20	Facilitate international money transfer	As a GS Online Banking user on the IMT Transfer details screen, I want to proceed to the next screen, so that I can confirm the details entered for the international transfer.	1	1
IMT-21	Facilitate international money transfer	As a GS Online Banking user on the IMT Transfer confirmation screen, I want to see the Total amount that will be transferred, so that I confirm the amount before final transfer.	2	2
IMT-22	Facilitate international money transfer	As a GS Online Banking user on the IMT Transfer confirmation screen, I want to see the selected debit account, so that I confirm the account details before final transfer.	2	2
IMT-23	Facilitate international money transfer	As a GS Online Banking user on the IMT Transfer confirmation screen, I want to see the beneficiary account, so that I confirm the beneficiary account details before final transfer.	2	2
IMT-24	Facilitate international money transfer	As a GS Online Banking user on the IMT Transfer confirmation screen, I want to see the payment date & disclaimer, so that I am aware when the beneficiary will receive the payment.	3	3
IMT-25	Facilitate international money transfer	As a GS Online Banking user on the IMT Confirmation screen, I want an option to go back to the International Transfer detail screen, so that I can modify the previously entered details.	3	3
IMT-26	Facilitate international money transfer	As a GS Online Banking user on the IMT Transfer Confirmation screen, I want to proceed to the next screen, so that I can confirm the details entered for the international transfer	1	2
IMT-27	Facilitate international money transfer	As a GS Online Banking user on the Transfer Receipt screen, I want to see the final transfer details, so that I can keep the receipt for my records.	2	3
IMT-28	Facilitate international money transfer	As a GS Online Banking user on the Transfer Receipt screen, I want to see a receipt number for my transfer, so that I can use it for tracking the transfer	2	3
IMT-29	Facilitate international money transfer	As a GS Online Banking user on the Transfer Receipt screen, I want to have an option to print the confirmation details., so that I keep a receipt of transfer for tracking and future reference	4	3

User Story #	Feature	User Story details	Priority	Risk Rating
IMT-30	Error handling for transfer screens	As a GS Online Banking user on the IMT main screen, I want to see an appropriate error message if the entered account number or IBAN is invalid, so that I can modify it before the transfer	2	3
IMT-31	Error handling for transfer screens	As a GS Online Banking user on the IMT main screen, I want to see an appropriate error message if the entered SWIFT code is invalid, so that I can modify it before the transfer	2	3
IMT-32	Error handling for transfer screens	As a GS Online Banking user on the IMT Transfer details screen, I want to see an appropriate error message if I have entered amount which is not in the range specified by the bank, so that I can modify the amount to be in range.	2	2
IMT-33	Error handling for transfer screens	As a GS Online Banking user on the IMT Transfer details screen, I want to see an appropriate error message if the total cost is greater than my account balance, so that I can change the transfer amount.	1	1
IMT-34	Error handling for transfer screens	As a GS Online Banking user on the IMT Transfer details screen, I want to see an appropriate error message if I have missed to enter any of the mandatory detail, so that I can enter them now.	2	2
IMT-35	Error handling for transfer screens	As a GS Online Banking user on the IMT Transfer details screen, I want to see an appropriate error message if I have not acknowledged the terms and conditions for the transfer, so that I read and acknowledge them.	2	2
IMT-36	Customer receives the Transfer confirmation	As a GS Online Banking user who has completed an international transfer, I want to receive the receipt of my transfer to my email, which I have provided to the bank, so that I can use that for tracking and future reference.	4	3
IMT-37	Customer receives the Transfer confirmation	As a GS Online Banking user who has completed an international transfer, I want to receive the receipt of my transfer as a notification to my internet banking mailbox, so that I can use that for tracking and future reference.	3	3
IMT-38	Account Balances after the transfer	As a GS Online Banking user who has completed an international transfer, my account balance must be updated, so that I am aware of my current balance immediately after the transfer.	1	1

2. Specify the definition of "DONE"

In Agile Software Development, we use the User Story Definition Of Done (DOD) to ensure the quality of work and to assess whether the team can consider the user story to be complete and ready for shipping to the customer. The story can be marked only as Done when ALL of the criteria defined in DOD are met. For IMT project the team has decided following as DOD:

- Coding completed
- Code peer-reviewed
- The unit tests were written, automated, executed, and passed
- The user story has been reviewed by team
- Every acceptance criteria have at least a test case associated
- Integration testing performed and compiles
- Functional tests passed
- Acceptance tests completed
- The product Owner reviewed the test results and approved

3. Create an initial system architecture

The system architecture diagram is the pictorial representation of the system with details of the internal component with high-level interactions and dataflow. It shows how different components are connected and the connectivity with any external systems. These diagrams are prepared by system architects or designers and are part of the initial design document. These documents help the developer in understanding the overall development work at a high-level. Using these document Testing team members can get a clear picture of the overall system, which is useful while creating the test strategy and test plan. Testers' can also use this to plan for their system integration tests and understand the downstream system risks. (how the data flow from this system can affect the other applications which are using it as an input)

The following diagrams show the current state of the Global Sun online banking system.

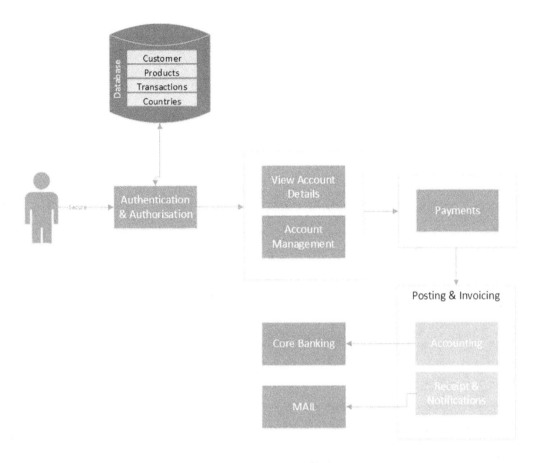

CURRENT STATE

The following diagrams show the high-level future state for the Global Sun online banking system after IMT changes:

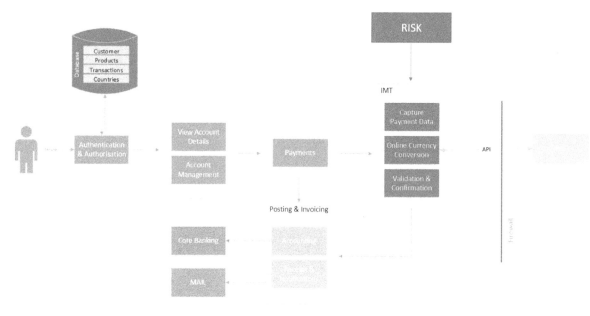

FUTURE STATE AFTER IMT CHANGES

Note
The new IMT system will get data-feed from an internal Global Sun system called RISK which will send the data for the list of countries on the sanctions list (not eligible for international transfers), the minimum and maximum limit for transfers and UpToDate terms and conditions, etc. This information will come to the RISK system from other systems or entered manually by the RISK system team.
The New IMT system is also connected to the SWIFT system. The current currency exchange rates are received in real-time from SWIFT and once the customer confirms the international payment it is converted to a SWIFT message and sent to the SWIFT system which acts as a network for the financial institutions.

The detailed design phase will go along with individual sprints where the next level of details will be identified, such as-

1. **Capture Payment Data**

   - Form design to capture customer and payment data
   - Design approvals from PO, UX team for identified data elements
   - Field data validation for individual fields
   - Database design
   - End to end sequence diagram design
   - Securing the data during transit and data at rest

2. **Online Currency Conversion**

   - Detailed interface design to interact with external API.
   - Infrastructure design to access the external resources outside of the organisation.
   - Design of end to end security layer to securely transfer the data to API.
   - Request/response model design
   - Exception handling, logging, and monitoring design

3. **Validation & Confirmation**

   - Form design shows the output and receives the customer confirmation
   - Design approvals from PO, UX team for identified data elements
   - Field data validation for individual fields
   - Database design
   - End to end sequence diagram design
   - Securing the data during transit and data at rest
   - Notification to the customer via email

Note
In large Agile projects during Sprint Zero, only the high-level design is prepared. This design is detailed and improvised during the subsequent sprints. This allows the team to have flexibility when there are changes required later in the project.

4. Undertake quality risk analysis

As discussed in chapter 12, the team has gone through the exercise of risk identification and categorization and identified the following risks that could affect product quality.

Risk	Probability	Impact
1234 – New IMT functionality can impact the existing functionality of online banking	Medium	High
1235- SWIFT currency rate is not updated in the IMT system	High	High
1236-Customer can transfer more than their account balance	High	High
1237-Customer can transfer money to Sanctions Risk list (SRL) countries	Low	High

Note
During the sprint, the team will discuss each story to discuss any product risk associated with the story.

5. Create an initial Test Strategy and Test Plan

As testers are part of the Agile team and their testing effort is visible to the entire team, lightweight work product documentation is suitable for any work product creation. Both Test Strategy and Test Plan focus on only the necessary information, excluding the extra information that may already be part of the project plan or any other document.

Test Strategy explains the overall test approach, which is not very project specific so it can be used across different projects.

Below is the Test Strategy for the online banking program on the program confluence (wiki) page, the same is used for the IMT project:

`https://confluence/Online-banking/Test-Strategy`

Test Strategy

Version:	1.0
Date	01/01/XXXX
Release State:	Final
Prepared by:	Test Manager

Purpose of document

This Testing Strategy document aims to provide an overview of the testing and automation approach for the relevant stakeholders.

Test Approach

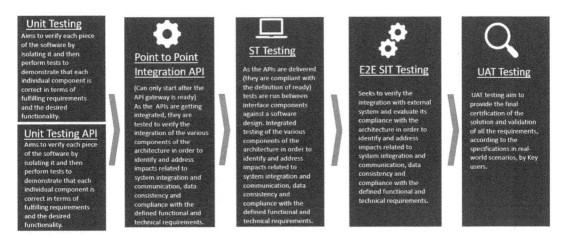

Test Automation

The below diagram outlines the test types, the focus of automated test development, and how they are leveraged within the CI/CD pipeline.

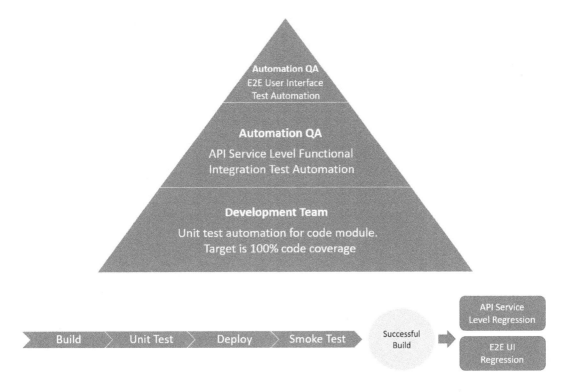

Test Types

Automation Test Suite	Run frequency
Unit Testing – Component level tests automated by the development team to ensure individual modules of code are functioning as expected before the build is deployed.	Before every build deploy (Integrated to CI pipeline)
Smoke Test – Small targeted regression suite aimed at verifying core components and integration is available.	Every morning on each environment (Scheduled) After every successful build deploy
API Service Level – Part of the full regression suite, aimed at validating all functional integration.	Every morning on each environment (Scheduled)
End-to-end User Interface - Part of the full regression suite, aimed at validating all core user journeys. Tests are initiated from the user interface and exercise the full E2E flow.	Every morning on each environment (Scheduled)

Test Tools

Test Tools	Description
JIRA	User story, defect, test case management, and reporting tool
Confluence	Document creation and repository
Test automation will be developed and run using the Global Sun automation framework consisting of: • Robot Framework • Jenkins • Selenium • AWS configured servers	Applications used to automate and run functional test cases

Test Environment:

To run different test phases following test environments are required.

Environment	Description
DEV	An isolated environment used by development team for development, component, component integration testing and automation activities. Each project will maintain its own instance of dev environment.
TEST	User story testing
SIT	• System Testing • System Integration Testing • Regression Testing
UAT	UAT testing

Defect Management

Defects identified during test execution may affect multiple components as well as time frames. This will require a formal and disciplined approach in the Defect resolutions process to ensure timely deliverables. The Test Lead will oversee the Defect Management Processes and lead the Defect Triage Meetings with the help of project testers across all phases of testing.

The project will follow the below guidelines for defect management across all the test phases:

- All defects will be logged in JIRA
- Release specific JIRA labels will be used to group the defects by project release

Defect Logging

JIRA will be used to log defects. All project team members will be provided access to JIRA so that they can log and/or access defects. The Test Lead will facilitate an initial "triage" activity with nominated Business resources whereby all defects are evaluated and assessed for completeness/appropriateness.

Defect workflow

Following Global Sun enterprise Bug workflow will be followed in JIRA and will be used to perform periodic triage of defects.

Defect Severity

Severity	Description	Description of Severity
1	Critical	Showstopper. The system cannot run or perform a major function. The testing of subsequent functions cannot be performed. Fixing the problem is critical for the acceptance of the system. Testing cannot continue, or the majority of test scripts would be invalidated if testing continued.
2	Major	A major function provides incorrect information or cannot be assessed. A minor function provides an incorrect result, and no suitable workaround exists. Testing can continue. Testing of impaired function and related function is impacted.
3	Minor	Low priority problems. Minor functions that provide an incorrect result should be resolved, but a workaround exists. Testing can continue. May invalidate a localized group of test scripts/steps.

Severity	Description	Description of Severity
4	Low	Cosmetic or similar errors that do not impact the functionality or performance of the system but should be resolved. All testing can continue. Only test scripts specifically testing the problem affected.

Defect Triage meeting

Defect review meetings will be conducted daily by the Test Lead during the test execution window along with all relevant stakeholders. The primary responsibility of such meetings will be to:

- Agree that recorded incidents are valid defects or not
- Agree on severity and priority of defects
- Agree to close defects
- Track progress of defect resolution process

Assess impact to test schedule and recommend action plan as required

Approve migration of defect fixes outside normally scheduled migration window depending on criticality and severity of the defect. Migrations will be balanced with other projects and outages agreed at the E2E Test Manager forum meetings.

The Project Manager, Test Lead, Testers, Business Analyst, Product Owner/Business tester, Development team will attend defect review meetings. In the event that the resolution of a Defect cannot be agreed upon during the course of the normal defect review meetings, the defect will be escalated to the Project Manager, who will convene an appropriate group for decision making.

Note

This Test Strategy is for the Global Sun online banking portfolio, and the team is using the same for the IMT project. As we can see, this test strategy is relatively lightweight as compared to the Test Strategy created for sequential development. In Agile projects, a test strategy is a static document that doesn't change much over time. This document is more of a guide for the teams to understand how the test processes work in an organization or portfolio.

Below is the Test Plan created for the IMT project on the project confluence (wiki) page:

https://confluence/IMT-Project/Test-Plan

Test Plan

Version:	1.0
Date	04/01/XXXX
Release State:	Final
Prepared by:	Tester

Introduction

This Test plan is a baseline to identify the scope for testing for IMT project and discuss the risks and assumptions

For more details about the IMT project please check **https://confluence/IMT-project**

Test Objectives

The primary objectives of testing are to validate:

- New IMT functionality is working as per the specifications
- The business functionality of Online Banking is working as per the previous release R2.2

In Scope

Testing of all the new functionality created as part of IMT project, regression testing for the identified high-risk areas for Online banking, and UAT testing.

Out of Scope

load testing is not required for this release as the existing customers will be using the IMT functionality, and the bank doesn't see a surge of new customers due to the IMT project.

Resourcing:

Two testing resources are working on the IMT project for sprint testing. One tester will be working 100% from the start of the project, and an automation tester will be working 50% from the start of sprint-1.

New functionality testing

Feature Description	High-level Testing details
Entitlements for IMT eligible customers	This will be tested for all the existing customer types on all supported browsers.
Facilitate international transfer	In-depth testing will be done on all supported browsers.
Error handling for transfer screens	In-depth testing will be done to verify all the error messages on all supported browsers.
The customer receives a Transfer confirmation	As the TEST environment is not connected to the email server, we cannot test that the email is sent to the customer's external email id after the transfer is successful. Therefore, the scope of testing will be to check that the message is there in the online banking mailbox.
Account Balances after the transfer	Extensive testing will be done to make sure that account balances are updated in real-time, and the customers can't transfer more than their account balance.

End to End testing

This testing will be done by the IMT project testers in the integrated SIT environment after the end of all the sprints. Selected tests will be run end to end to ensure the successful integration of all the features and continuity between components developed by different teams.

Regression Testing

All the identified high-risk Regression Test scripts will be executed to verify the existing Online Banking functionality. Automation scripts will be used for some of the targeted regression.

UAT testing

UAT testing will be performed and coordinated by the business team after the end-to-end testing. This testing will validate that the system is complete and is working as expected.

Assumptions

Assumption	Impact (If Assumption is Incorrect)	Responsible	Confirmed by date
The TEST environment is available for the IMT Project from the start of the first iteration. (from 23rd MAR YYYY)	Testing activity for sprints can't start	Test Manager	15 Mar YYYY
All required test data is present in the test environment	The start of the test phase will not be achievable	Test Manager	19 Mar YYYY

Infrastructure Requirements

Existing online banking test environments will be used for testing.

Online banking **"TEST"** environment will be used for:

- User story testing

Online banking **"SIT"** environment will be used for:

- End to End testing
- Regression testing

Each environment will interface to the RISK and SWIFT simulator.

Online banking **"UAT"** environment will be used for:

- End to End testing
- UAT Testing

This environment will interface with the RISK and SWIFT test systems.

Note
For integration testing, there is a possibility that one of the external systems is not ready or not accessible for testing. In this case, simulators are used to mimic these external systems. A Simulator is a device, computer program, or system used during testing, which behaves or operates like a given system when provided with a set of controlled inputs.

Risks

At the time of the initial release of this document, the following project risks have been identified that could affect the release date.

Risk	Impact	Probability	Mitigation
1010- E2E Testing is not completed on time due to late delivery or data/ environment issues	High	Low	Extra testing resources from the banking portfolio can be used as a contingency to complete testing.

The following have been identified as risks that could affect product quality

Risk	Impact	Probability	Mitigation
1234 - New IMT functionality can impact the existing functionality of online banking	High	Medium	Targeted regression testing of online banking will be done after the system testing of IMT is complete
1235- SWIFT currency rate is not updated in the IMT system	High	High	Extensive Integration testing with the system providing currency rates will be done during E2E testing. Testing will be done to prove that the IMT transfers can't happen if the rates are not updated every 30 mins.
1236-Customer can transfer more than their account balance	High	High	Testing will be done to prove that the IMT transfers can't happen if the customer is trying to transfer more than their account balance.
1237-Customer can transfer money to Sanctions Risk list (SRL) countries	High	Low	Testing will be done to prove that the Sanction list countries are not appearing in the dropdown list for bank locations and beneficiary address country, and the list is accessed real-time from the RISK system.

Note
During sprint zero, the team will also undertake following task: • Create the Agile task board • Procure and install required tools for test management, defect management, test automation, and continuous integration. • Define test metrics to measure the test process, the progress of testing in the project and product quality

Sprint-1

Sprint-1 is the first development iteration of the project. The Scrum team (Product owner, Testers, Developers, BA, Scrum Master) will now actively participate in all the sprint ceremonies. One of the first tasks for the Scrum team is to create the Sprint backlog. It is a list of all the user stories and tasks which are to be worked upon in a particular sprint. Sprint backlog is the subset of Product backlog and is owned by the Scrum Team. It is created during the Sprint planning.

Sprint planning

Sprint planning meeting happens at the beginning of a new sprint. In this meeting, the Scrum Team identifies the User Stories for the current sprint and then, with the Product Owner's help, understands them and adds these to the sprint backlog. The Scrum team will pick the story from the product backlog based on the priority and risk rating. The highest priority and highest risk rating will be worked first unless that story is dependent on any other story. Based on these criteria, the team has first picked IMT-01 which is to check customer entitlements for IMT transfers.

Story IMT-01
As an authorized GS online banking user
for International transfers,
I want to have a menu option,
so that I can initiate an international transfer.

First, the Product Owner will describe this story's business value to the team, and then the team will start the discussion on this story.

Product Owner: " The main goal of the story is to provide an option for the customer to go to the IMT screen. Once the customer has logged in to the online banking site, we can provide them a menu option for IMT transfer in the Account landing page."

Developer-1: " In Account page, we already have a menu for Fund transfer. I think it will be good if we can add the menu for IMT there."

Product Owner: "Yes, I agree. It will be consistent for the user; they can see all the Fund transfer options in one place."

Tester: "Can all the customers see this IMT option once they login in?"

Product Owner: "No, it is only there for the customer who is entitled to do international transfers; the customer has to contact the bank to get registered for IMT transfer. Also, the customer who has at least one transaction account been provided with this option."

Tester: "What is the requirement around at least having one transaction account?"

Product Owner: "The customer can make an international transfer only from a transaction account, so if they don't have a transaction account, they can't register for IMT transfer."

Tester: "Then we need to verify that a customer who is already entitled to IMT transfer can't see this option once they close their transaction account."

Product Owner: "Yes, this is a good check."

Tester: "Can the customer who is registered for IMT transfer contact the bank to deregister them?"

Product Owner: "Yes, then the menu option should not be there for them."

Tester: "How can we test that once the user clicks on the new menu item, they are transferred to the transfer page as the New International Transfer page is not ready?"

Developer-2: "We will create a mock New International Transfer page; it will just show the layout with no functionality."

Business Analyst: "If everybody is clear, then we can formulate the acceptance criteria for this User Story."

All agreed, and the team started formulating the acceptance criteria.

Story IMT-01

As an authorized online banking user for International transfers,

I want to have a menu option,

so that I can initiate an international transfer.

AC-1

Given: The user entitled for International transfer has logged in to the GS Online Banking page & is on the Account landing page.

When: The user hovers on the 'Fund transfer' menu item

Then: The user can see a "New International Transfer" menu after "New multiple funds transfer."

AC-2

Given: The user not entitled to International transfer has logged in to the GS Online Banking page & is on the Account landing page.

When: The user hovers on the 'Fund transfer' menu item

Then: The user is not able to see the "New International Transfer" menu

AC-3

Given: The user entitled for International transfer has logged in to the GS Online Banking page & is on the Account landing page.

When: The user clicks on the "New International Transfer" menu under 'Fund transfer.'

Then: The user should be navigated to the New International Transfer page.

AC-4

Given: The user entitled for International transfer has closed all their transactions accounts.

When: The user clicks on the 'Fund transfer' menu item

Then: The user is not able to see the "New International Transfer" menu

AC-5

Given: The user entitled for International transfer has deregistered from International transfers.

When: The user clicks on the 'Fund transfer' menu item

Then: The user is not able to see the "New International Transfer" menu

---

Note
As we can see how based on the discussion between the team members, a lot of new things about the story came to light and got clarified. Now all the team has the same understanding of the story. As the team is writing the acceptance criteria together, all the team members are crystal clear about the customer requirements. With all this additional information, the team can do a proper estimate or sizing of the story. In some of the projects, the Product Owner and BA will create the initial Acceptance criteria and then the team will refine and extend them during the planning session.

Estimation

Once the team is clear about the purpose of the story and the business value, the Scrum Master will call for a team estimate. Each team member privately selects one card from the deck of Planning Poker cards. These cards have the following values to represent their estimated story points.

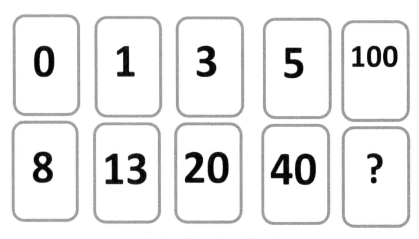

Poker Planning Cards

Now all the team members will reveal the card. Developer-1 holds up a 5 card, developer-2 holds up an 8 card, and the tester holds up a 13 card.

Developer-1   Developer-2   Tester

Generally, for unequal estimation values, a discussion is started; usually, the team member with the highest and the lowest value will provide their reasoning.

Scrum Master: "Developer-1, why did you choose 5?"

Developer-1: "We already have the entitlements functionality for the 'New multiple fund transfer' I think we can reuse most of the code for our development?"

Developer-2: "No, the 'New multiple fund transfer' is applicable for all the customers; we can't reuse that for IMT."

Developer-1: "I was not sure about this. In this case, I agree with developer 2. The effort will be more than what I initially anticipated."

Scrum Master: "Tester, why did you choose 13?"

Tester: "We have to verify the new menu is there and showing up properly on all the different browsers supported for the online banking site."

Developer-2: "I agree, the testing effort is more as we have to test with a different set of customers and on different browsers."

Scrum Master: "Can we have another round based on this additional information."

In the second-round team agrees on the size of the story as **13**.

On many occasions, the story can require a lot of testing effort, and the coding effort is relatively small. At other times, the reverse can also happen. Therefore, it is crucial to consider all the perspectives.

Now the team will pick the next story from the backlog based on the priority and risk.

Story IMT-03
As a GS online Banking user on the IMT main screen,
I want the list of eligible countries to be populated,
so that I can select the Beneficiary's bank location
from the list.

Product Owner: "The main goal of the user story is to provide the customer with a dropdown with a list of countries eligible for international transfer."

Developer-2: "What is the source for this list of eligible countries?"

Product Owner: "IMT system should get the list from the RISK System. Eligible countries list is maintained in RISK System."

Tester: "Are we going to access the country list in real-time?"

Product Owner: "Yes, it should be a real-time call once the user is on the IMT transfer page."

Developer-1: "For the story IMT-06, we are also using the same API to call the eligible country list; we can include that story in the Sprint. There will be a little development work, but the testing effort will be there."

Story IMT-06
As a GS online Banking user on the IMT main screen
I want the eligible list of countries to be populated
under Beneficiary's details, so that I can select the
beneficiary's country of location

Scrum Master: "I agree, as it is similar functionality, let us develop and test it together.

Tester: "How will we test it as the IMT main screen UI is not ready yet?".

Developer-2: "As we don't have the User Interface (UI) ready for IMT main screen, we will just test the API calls to verify that the functionality is working fine."

Business Analyst: "If everybody is clear, then we can formulate the acceptance criteria for both the stories."

API Testing

API (Application Programming Interface) is a software solution or collection of functions that allows systems and applications to communicate with each other. The end-user interacts with the UI on top and is usually never aware that an API exists underneath.

An API protocol defines the rules for API calls: it specifies accepted data types and commands. Different API architectures specify different protocol constraints.

REST (Representational State Transfer) is a popular web API architecture. To be a REST API, an API must adhere to certain architectural constraints or principles. Consumers of these APIs are capable of sending different verbs. Generally, the four primary HTTP verbs are used as follows:

- **GET**- Read a specific resource (by an identifier) or a collection of resources.
- **PUT** -Update a specific resource (by an identifier) or a collection of resources.
- **DELETE** -Remove/delete a specific resource by an identifier.
- **POST** -Create a new resource.

Each API call has a specific function with a number of parameters that can accept different inputs, and a variation of these inputs will return a different result. While testing APIs, testers rely on the status code which API returns. If the request is successful, the status code is 200,2xx, or if there was something wrong with the request, the status code is 4xx, or if something went wrong in the server application, the call would return the status code of 5xx.

As we have seen from **story IMT-03/IMT-06**, these APIs can be developed early in the development cycle. This means that the testing for these stories can be completed early, even before the UI is developed. Also, these API tests can be automated easily.

Story IMT-03

As a GS Online Banking user on the IMT main screen,

I want the list of eligible countries to be populated,

so that I can select the Beneficiary's bank location from the list.

AC-1

Given: The user has clicked on the "New International Transfer" menu and is on the New International Transfer page.

When: The user checks the "Beneficiary's bank location" dropdown

Then: The dropdown should have the same list of countries eligible for international transfer as in the RISK system.

AC-2

Given: The user has clicked on the "New International Transfer" menu and is on the New International Transfer page.

When: User select a location from the "Beneficiary's bank location" dropdown

Then: The user selection is highlighted and displayed in the field.

Story IMT-06

As a GS Online Banking user on the IMT main screen,

I want the eligible list of countries to be populated under the Beneficiary's details,

so that I can select the beneficiary's country of location.

AC-1

Given: User has clicked on the "New International Transfer" menu and is on the New International Transfer page

When: The user checks the "Beneficiary's address country" dropdown

Then: The dropdown should have the same list of countries eligible for international transfer as in the RISK system

AC-2

Given: User has clicked on the "New International Transfer" menu and is on the New International Transfer page

When: User select a location from the "Beneficiary's address country" dropdown

Then: The user selection is highlighted and displayed in the field.

Estimation

The team agrees on the story's size as 20 for IMT-03 because there is a lot of development effort in building a new API to fetch the data from the RISK system.

The team agrees on 3 story point for IMT-06. This is based on the fact that most of the IMT-06 functionality development will be covered as part of IMT-03; the testing effort will still be there.

Creating Task Cards

The team has decided to go with these three stories in this Sprint. Now they can start creating the development and testing task for these stories. The coding task includes coding, unit testing, and automation of unit test cases. The testing task includes test case preparation, execution effort. Some teams include automation of the test cases in testing tasks or create a separate ticket to track that. Generally, the team tries to identify the test data required during the Sprint zero and ensure that they have it before the Sprint. Initially, both the dev and test task cards will be in the "To do" column and then will move according to the progress made by team members. The development card will stay in the "In Test" column until the testing task has been completed. Both these cards will move to the "Done" column simultaneously once the Product Owner is happy with the story.

Daily Scrum (Daily Stand-up)

Now, as the team members have created the task and working on them, they will provide the update on these tasks during the daily stand-up. The Scrum Master, the Product Owner, or any Stakeholder may attend as listeners. When the teams are co-located, the stand-up is mostly done near the Agile board (Agile Wall), so the other attendees know which tasks the team members are referring to. For distributed teams, a virtual Agile board may be helpful during the stand-up.

Below is the conversation from the stand-up meeting from day-6 of Sprint.

Developer 1:   "Yesterday, I completed coding for story IMT-03".

"Today, I will be continuing on the unit testing, and hopefully, by the end of the day, the story should be ready for testing."

"No blockers."

Tester: "Yesterday, I finished the test case preparation for the IMT-03".

"Today, I will start testing of IMT-01 as it is ready for testing".

"I still don't have access to the RISK system, and if this is not resolved, it can block the testing of IMT-03".

Scrum Master: "Why do you need access to RISK System."

Tester: "I have test scenario where I have to update the eligible country list in RISK and see if it reflected in the API call".

Scrum Master: "OK, leave it on me; I will liaise with the RISK team and get the access issue sorted by today."

Developer 2:   "Yesterday, I finished the task related to the development for story IMT-01".

"Today, I will support developer-1 on automating the unit test for IMT-03."

Scrum Master: "Any impediments."

Developer 2:   "No."

Scrum Master: "OK, great. We are making good progress."

Testing activities for Sprint-1

The testing activities for Sprint include test case preparation, automation, and execution. As there are three stories included for the Sprint, the testers will prepare the test cases for them while development activities are going on.

Test cases preparation:

While the high-level test cases are already created as part of acceptance criteria, the tester may create detailed test cases that can be used for current user story testing and end-to-end testing when the entire application is ready. Most of them will be automated by the automation tester as well.

IMT-01 test cases

TC ID	TC Name	REF	Step No.	Test Step Description	Expected Results
TC_01.01	Verify IMT Menu_1	IMT-01	PREQ	User entitled for International transfer has logged in to GS Online Banking page.	The user is on the Account landing page
			Step1	User hover on 'Fund transfer' menu item	User can see a **"New International Transfer"** menu after "New multiple funds transfer"
TC_01.02	Verify IMT Menu_2	IMT-01	PREQ	User not entitled (not registered, deregistered, no transactions acc.) International transfer has logged in to the GS Online Banking page	The user is on the Account landing page
			Step1	User hover on 'Fund transfer' menu item	The user is not able to see the **"New International Transfer"** menu
TC_01.03	Verify IMT Menu_3	IMT-01	PREQ	User entitled for International transfer has logged in to the GS Online Banking page	The user is on the Account landing page
			Step1	User hover on 'Fund transfer' menu item	User can see a **"New International Transfer"** menu after "New multiple funds transfer"
			Step2	User click on **"New International Transfer"** menu	User should be navigated to New International Transfer page

Dealing with Defects

During the test execution for the above story, the tester has noticed that the international money transfer link is not displaying for a basic access account customer type. In this case, the tester can quickly show this issue to the developer to be sure that it is not an issue with test data or the environment. Once agreed, the tester can now create a defect with minimal documentation as the developer has already seen the issue. The lean documentation principle of Agile is applicable for defects also. The tester will create a new defect task which will become part of the sprint backlog. This task will move like any other development task.

Defect # 11

User is not able to see IMT link for the customer with basic access account entitled for IMT transfers

The tester will also raise this defect in the defect management system (JIRA) for tracking purpose:

Defect ID	Defect #11
Severity	Critical
Data Raised	12-Jan-xxxx
Summary	User is not able to see IMT link for the customer with basic access account entitled for IMT transfers
Reference	Story IMT-01
Test data	**Customer id**: B501241, **Password**: Passw@rd123

IMT-03 test cases

TC ID	TC Name	Test objective	Step No.	Test Step Description	Expected Results
TC_03.01	Verify Beneficiary bank countries	To verify that the user can select a country from the beneficiary bank location dropdown	PREQ	Enter Request URL in Postman and click on the send button	
			Step1	Check the response	Status should be 200 OK, and All the eligible countries should be displayed in the response

IMT-06 test cases

TC ID	TC Name	Test objective	Step No.	Test Step Description	Expected Results
TC_06.01	Verify Beneficiary countries	To verify the user can select a country from the beneficiary address from location dropdown	PREQ	Enter Request URL in Postman and click on the send button	
			Step1	Check the response	Status should be 200 OK, and All the eligible countries should be displayed in the response.

While testing, the tester will check whether all the eligible countries from the RISK system are there in the API response. The API response will look something like this:

```
{
    "status": "OK",
    "status-code": 200,
    "total": 105,

    "data": {
        "DZ": {
            "country": "Algeria",
            "region": "Africa"
        },
        "AO": {
            "country": "Angola",
            "region": "Africa"
        },
        .........
    }
}
```

Note
Apart from the test cases, there will be additional test cases to check that when the eligible country list is changed in RISK, it is reflected in the new response. After running all the test cases created for the story, the testers will also do some **exploratory testing** to test the critical areas using session-based testing. These sessions are defined as an uninterrupted period of testing which could last from 60 to 120 minutes.

Sprint Review/ Iteration Review/Showcase /Demo

At the End of the Sprint, the team gets a chance to show the complete stories to the Product Owner, members of the customer team and other stakeholders. As they can see the working software, they can ask relevant questions and provide real-time feedback. The team drives the showcase, but the Product Owner can ask for different scenarios to be demonstrated to get confidence about the developed functionality/feature. The sprint review is a good opportunity for the team to show what they have completed and get feedback that can be used for current and future iterations. Generally, the testers or BA will run the sprint review as they have worked on the stories and have a good idea of what the customers need to know about the new functionality.

Below is the conversation from the sprint review.

Tester: "I will start with the demo of IMT-01 to check the entitlement for the IMT users; let me run the happy flow to show you the new menu."

After the demo...

Business SME 1: "Looks good. Can we try one of these scenarios where the customer has deregistered for IMT and then see the link is there?"

Tester: "As you know, deregistration is only effective in the system the next day after the end-of-day batch is run. I have tested that already, and I can show the test results"?

Business SME 1: "OK great, can we try with one on the happy flow with one of the joint accounts."

Tester: "Sure, we can try it out?"

Business SME 2: "Can we try it for Youth account- where the customer age is less than 18, IMT link should not be there."

Developer 1: "We have not catered for this; there was no requirement around this."

Product owner: "Yes, that is correct; I was under the impression that youth account holders can't register for IMT."

Business SME 2: "They can register but can't do IMT transfer. Once they turn 18, we will automatically change their account to a normal account with all functionality."

Product Owner: "OK, it is an important one then. Can we include that in our acceptance criteria?"

Business Analyst: "Sure, can this be completed by the end of the sprint."

Developer 1: "It is a small change I can do that."

Tester: "I can show the functionality of IMT-03/IMT-06. In both we are checking the country list for beneficiary bank location and beneficiary country is picked correctly from the RISK system. I will use the API calls to show that all the eligible countries are picked from the RISK system."

After the demo...

Business SME 3: "Looks good to me, but what if the customer has selected the country and they are on the next page? Meanwhile, the country is blacklisted and not eligible for transfer"?

Developer 2: "I think we can do a final check for the country when the user clicks on the final submit button."

Product Owner: "I think that will be good. I will create a new story to track that."

Business Analyst: "I have created story IMT-39 and added to the product backlog."

Scrum Master: "We can move IMT-03 and IMT-06 to the "Done" column now. We will wait for IMT-01 changes to be developed and tested."

Note
Although the Product Owner is actively involved throughout the Sprint to provide feedback, when the team shows the working software with limited capability to a wider customer group and business SME, it opens up a dialog with them. It helps to detect any potential issues with the system. This exercise is also helpful for development for future sprints as, after these conversations, the team knows the customer better and knows what they are looking for in the system.

Sprint Retrospective

Agile teams strive to continuously improve the way they work. Retrospectives allow the team to identify what and how they can work better. As this meeting happens at the end of each sprint, this provides an excellent opportunity to look back at the sprint to check what went well, what didn't, and what the team can do in the future sprints to incorporate the improvements and retain the successes. There are different approaches to conduct retrospectives, but all of them have a common theme of having a safe environment of mutual trust and respect to make the process better without targeting or blaming anyone for the team failures.

The team may invite other stakeholders to participate to make this a successful meeting. All participants can provide input on both testing and non-testing activities.

One of the simple and common exercises used in the retrospective is to use "**what went well**" and "**what could be improved**" exercises. The team can use either a digital whiteboard or a physical one, Scrum Master, or the team member who is facilitating the meeting, will create three columns with the headings "What went well," "What could be improved," and "Actions." Then the team is given a set amount of time (10-15 mins) to think and write down their observation (one idea per note) about the Sprint as they relate to the following categories:

What went well: Actions we should keep doing and formalize

What could be improved: Actions we should start taking or prevent/remove

When everyone is done, the facilitator, with the help of participates, group similar or duplicate ideas together. Then each idea is addressed one by one to allow people time to share input. At the end of the discussion, the team can set up a vote to decide which items are most important. Generally, each team member is given a chance to vote for a set number of items. The team can pick the items with the most votes (two to three) as the area of focus for the next Sprint. The team will brainstorm actions that can be taken to improve problem areas and write in the Actions column.

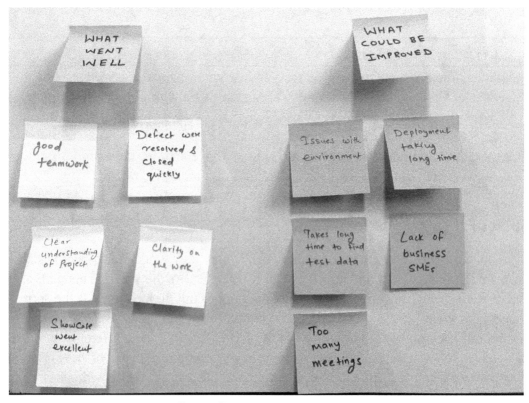

Sprint Retrospective exercise

Below are the ideas discussed during the Sprint-1 retrospective meeting:

What went well	votes
Collaboration- Good teamwork	5
Defect resolution- Defects were resolved and closed quickly	4
Showcase - Great flow and examples helped attendees understand the new developed functionality	3
Focused work – The Team is having clarity on the work and a clear understanding of the project	2

What could be improved	votes
Environment availability – Deployment taking a long time and environment not available for testing 1-2 hours every day	4
Test data – Finding the required data for testing taking a long time.	3
Meetings- Too many meetings hampering actual sprint work	5
Lack of access to Business SMEs- As there was no business SME for the RISK system, it has taken a long time to understand the system and update the countries eligible for IMT	3

Actions items

Item	Action	Owner
Environment availability – deployment taking a long time and environment not available for testing 1-2 hours every day	• Developer/Tester to collaborate • Developers will share the timelines for deployments in advance. • Change the schedule if testing is in progress.	Developer-1
Test data - Finding the required data for testing taking a long time	• The Product Owner will identify a business SME who can help the team in test data identification and verification.	Product Owner
Meetings- Too many meetings hampering actual sprint work	• All meetings should be with clear agenda & enough heads up. • No meetings between 11.00 am to 2.00 pm. • No meetings after 5.00 pm	Scrum Master
Lack of access to Business SMEs- As there was no business SME for the RISK system, it has taken a long time to understand the system and update the countries eligible for IMT	• Scrum Master to work with the RISK project manager to identify a business SME	Scrum Master

Note

There are many other ways to run a Retrospective meeting. Other examples include using the "Start, Stop, Continue" or "Good, Bad, Better, Best" exercises. The facilitator needs to create a column to represent each category, and team members can write their observations about the Sprint as they relate to the following categories:

Start: actions the team should start taking

Stop: actions the team should prevent or remove

Continue: actions the team should keep doing and formalize

OR

Good: Things that went well, i.e., areas where the team met or exceeded expectations

Bad: Things that didn't work well, i.e., areas where the team didn't meet expectations or where unexpected problems occurred

Better: Opportunities for improvement, i.e., suggestions on areas where the team can do something better

Best: Things that deserve recognition, i.e., exceptional teamwork or team member performance

Sprint Metrics

Agile metrics help the team to monitor their productivity and keep the team performance in check.

These metrics can help the team find their shortcoming in the initial stages, so they can take appropriate actions to work on these. The team has decided to use Sprint Burndown Chart & Velocity chart as the primary project metrics.

Below is the burndown chart for Sprint-1:

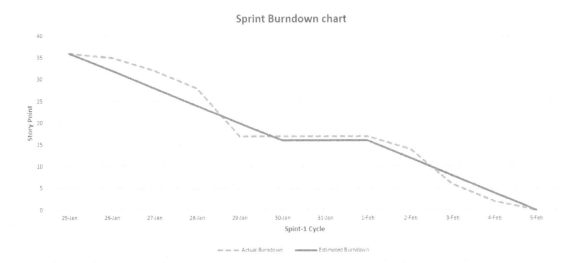

<table>
<tr><td>Note</td></tr>
</table>

The Sprint Burndown Chart makes the work of the team visible. It shows the rate at which work is completed and how much work remains to be done. As the development and testing for the story IMT-03 are completed mid-way of Sprint duration, the chart slopes downward. If the burndown line is not tracking downwards by mid-Sprint, the Scrum Master needs to quickly raise this flag and help the team to act early rather than drifting toward Sprint failure.

Sprint Burndown Chart is a very effective reporting tool in Agile projects as it shows Team progress towards the Sprint Goal, not in terms of time spent but in terms of how much work remains.

Below is the **velocity chart** for sprint-1:

Once the Sprint is completed, the Scrum Master will prepare the Velocity Chart. In Sprint 1 team estimated work for 36 story points and delivered work of 36 story points. Now the team velocity is established as 36 story points. For the next Sprint, the team can first pick work for 36 story points, and if they can finish it, they can pull more stories from the product backlog.

The velocity is ONLY considered for the stories which are moved into "Done" column during the Sprint. If the story is partially completed (e.g., dev completed but testing still pending), then the point related to that story cannot be added to velocity.

Example: By end of the Sprint-1, if the development of IMT-06 is completed but the testing is not finished. In this case, three-story points can't be added to sprint velocity, as IMT-06 is still not "Done." The velocity for the sprint will be considered as 33.

17 Subsequent Sprints

In subsequent Sprints, the team will pick the new stories from the product backlog or work on the stories which are remaining from the previous Sprints. Once the Sprint backlog is finalized, the team will perform all the Sprint ceremonies discussed in Sprint-1.

During the sprint, the tester will carry out the testing for the user stories selected for each sprint. Following test cases were created during the sprints for the remaining stories from the backlog.

IMT-02 - As a GS Online Banking user on IMT main screen, I want my eligible Accounts to be populated, so that I can select the account which can be used to initiate the transfer.

TC ID	TC Name	Objective	US Ref.	Step No.	Test Step Description	Expected Results
TC_01	Verify IMT Main Screen_1	To verify user accounts are populated on 'New International Transfer' main screen	IMT-02	PREQ	User has clicked on the **"New International Transfer"** menu and is on New International Transfer page	
				Step1	Verify the customer name	It is auto-populated and the same as the customer name from the online banking account page
TC_02	Verify_ IMT Main Screen_2	To verify that the user can select the eligible account as a from account for the International transfer	IMT-02	PREQ	User having a checking, saving, credit card, and a mortgage account has clicked on **"New International Transfer"** menu and is on New International Transfer page	
				Step1	Check the **"From account"** dropdown & select an account	• Only checking accounts should be there in the dropdown. The saving, mortgage account, and credit card should not be there in the dropdown. • The user is able to select an account from the dropdown.

IMT-04 - As a GS Online Banking user on the IMT main screen, I want Beneficiary's account details fields, so that I can enter the Beneficiary's bank account number or IBAN for International transfer and Beneficiary's Bank SWIFT/BIC code for International transfer

TC ID	TC Name	Objective	US Ref.	Step No.	Test Step Description	Expected Results
TC_03	Verify_ IMT Main Screen_3	To verify that the user can only enter a valid account number or IBAN in beneficiary bank details	IMT-04	PREQ	User has clicked on the "**New International Transfer**" menu and is on New International Transfer page	
				Step1	Try to enter the alphabets in the account number or IBAN field.	The field should not accept alphabets
				Step2	Try to enter an account number more than 12 digits	The field should not accept any digit after the 12th digit.
				Step3	Try to enter a valid account number which is 12 digits	The field should accept the account number.
TC_04	Verify IMT Main Screen_4	To verify that the user can only enter a valid SWIFT/BIC code in the bank SWIFT/BIC code field	IMT-04	PREQ	The user has clicked on the "**New International Transfer**" menu and is on the New International Transfer page	
				Step1	Try entering special characters in the SWIFT/BIC code field	The field should not accept special characters.
				Step2	Enter a SWIFT/BIC code with more than 12 digits	The field should not accept any digit after the 12th digit.
				Step3	Enter a valid SWIFT/BIC code e.g. USB-KUS44IMT	The field should accept the BIC code.

IMT-05 - As a GS Online Banking user on the IMT main screen, I want an option under Beneficiary's bank details, so that I can enter the beneficiary's name for International transfer.

TC ID	TC Name	Objective	US Ref.	Step No.	Test Step Description	Expected Results
TC_05	Verify IMT Main Screen_5	To verify that the user can enter a beneficiary name and validation for the field	IMT-05	PREQ	The user has clicked on the "**New International Transfer**" menu and is on New International Transfer page	
				Step1	Try to enter a Beneficiary's name with more than 25 characters	The field should not accept any new character after the 25th character.
				Step2	Try to enter a special character in the beneficiary's name field.

E.g., $ | User should not be able to enter any special characters in the name field |
| | | | | Step3 | Try to enter a digit in the beneficiary's name field.

E.g., 9 | User should not be able to enter any digit in the name field |
| | | | | Step4 | Try to enter a Beneficiary's name with spaces in the field | The field should accept the name |

IMT-07-As a GS Online Banking user on the IMT main screen, I want an option under Beneficiary's details, so that I can enter the beneficiary's primary address for International transfer

TC ID	TC Name	Objective	US Ref.	Step No.	Test Step Description	Expected Results
TC_06	Verify IMT Main screen_6	To verify the user can enter a primary address and validation for the field	IMT-07	PREQ	The user has clicked on the **"New International Transfer"** menu and is on New International Transfer page	
				Step1	Try to enter a primary address with more than 25 characters	The field should not accept any new character after the 25th character.
				Step2	Try to enter a special character in the beneficiary's name field. E.g., $	The field should accept the special characters
				Step3	Try to enter a digit in the beneficiary's name field. E.g., 9	The field should accept the digits
				Step4	Try to enter a primary address with spaces	The field should accept the address

IMT-08-As a GS Online Banking user on the IMT main screen, I want an option under Beneficiary's details, so that I can enter the beneficiary's secondary address for International transfer

TC ID	TC Name	Objective	US Ref.	Step No.	Test Step Description	Expected Results
TC_07	Verify IMT Main screen_7	To verify that the user can enter a second-ary address and validation for the field	IMT-08	PREQ	The user has clicked on the "**New International Transfer**" menu and is on the New International Transfer page	
				Step1	Try to enter a secondary address with more than 25 characters	The field should not accept any new character after the 25th character.
				Step2	Try to enter a special character in the benefi-ciary's name field. E.g. $	The field should accept the special characters
				Step3	Try to enter a digit in the beneficiary's name field. E.g., 9	The field should accept the digits
				Step4	Try to enter a secondary address with spaces	The field should accept the address

IMT-09 - As a GS Online Banking user on the IMT main screen, I want an option under Beneficiary's details, so that I can enter the message for the beneficiary for the International transfer.

TC ID	TC Name	Objective	US Ref.	Step No.	Test Step Description	Expected Results
TC_08	Verify IMT Main screen_8	To verify that the user can enter a message for the beneficiary and validation for the field	IMT-09	PREQ	The user has clicked on the "New International Transfer" menu and is on the New International Transfer page	
				Step1	Try to enter a Message to the beneficiary with more than 40 characters	The field should not accept any new character after the 40th character.
				Step2	Try to enter a special character in the Message to the beneficiary field. E.g., $	The field should accept the special characters
				Step3	Try to enter a digit in the message to the beneficiary field. E.g., 9	The field should accept the digits
				Step4	Try to enter a message to the beneficiary with spaces	The field should accept the message

IMT-10 - As a GS Online Banking user on the IMT main screen, I want an option under Beneficiary's details to enter description of transfer, so that I can see the details in my statement.

TC ID	TC Name	Objective	US Ref.	Step No.	Test Step Description	Expected Results
TC_09	Verify IMT Main screen_9	To verify the user can enter a description of transfer and validation for the field	IMT-10	PREQ	The user has clicked on the "New International Transfer" menu and is on the New International Transfer page	
				Step1	Try to enter a description of transfer with more than 20 characters	The field should not accept any new character after the 20th character.
				Step2	Try to enter a special character in description of transfer field.

E.g., $ | The field should accept the special characters |
| | | | | Step3 | Try to enter a digit in a description of transfer field.

E.g., 9 | The field should accept the digits |
| | | | | Step4 | Try to enter a description of transfer with spaces | The field should accept the message |

IMT-11 - As a GS Online Banking user on the IMT main screen, I must fill all the mandatory fields, so that I can proceed to the international transfer detail screen.

TC ID	TC Name	Objective	US Ref.	Step No.	Test Step Description	Expected Results
TC_10	Verify IMT Main screen_10	To verify that the user can proceed to Transfer detail page	IMT-11	PREQ	The user has clicked on the "**New International Transfer**" menu and is on the New International Transfer page	
				Step1	User has entered all the mandatory fields in the page and clicked on the Next button	The user is landed on the Transfer details page.

IMT-12 - As a GS Online Banking user on the IMT Transfer details screen, I want an option under Transfer details, so that I can enter the amount for the International transfer.

TC ID	TC Name	Objective	US Ref.	Step No.	Test Step Description	Expected Results
TC_11	Verify Transfer Detail screen_1	To verify that the user can enter the amount for transfer	IMT-12	PREQ	The user has completed all the details on the New International Transfer page and is on the Transfer details screen.	
				Step1	Try to enter a special character in the Amount field. E.g. -, $	The field should not allow entering special characters in the amount field
				Step2	Try to enter an alphabet in the **Amount** field. E.g., a, z	The field should not allow entering alphabet in the amount field
				Step3	Try to enter a digit in the **Amount** field. E.g., 100	The field should accept the digits

IMT-13 - As a GS Online Banking user on the IMT Transfer details screen, I want to see the amount including any additional fees associated for my international transfer, so that I aware of the Total cost for the transfer.

TC ID	TC Name	Objective	US Ref.	Step No.	Test Step Description	Expected Results
TC_12	Verify Transfer Detail screen_2	To verify the standard international fee is populated	IMT-13	PREQ	The user has completed all the details on the New International Transfer page and is on the Transfer details screen.	
				Step1	User has entered a valid amount in the Amount field	• The standard international fee is auto-populated. • The field is non-editable, and the value of the field should be the same as the standard international transfer fee from the RISK system.

IMT-14 - As a GS Online Banking user on the IMT Transfer details screen, I want to have an option to pay the fees for international transfer from my account or from transferred funds, so that I can select appropriate option.

TC ID	TC Name	Objective	US Ref.	Step No.	Test Step Description	Expected Results
TC_13	Verify Transfer Detail screen_3	To verify the option for paying the fees from account or transferred funds	IMT-14	PREQ	The user has completed all the details on the New International Transfer page and is on the Transfer details screen.	
				Step1	Check there is an option for paying the fees from account or transferred funds	• For the Fees will be deducted from field there should be a radio button for the "The account above" and "The funds, I'm sending" • The default value should be "The account above"

IMT-15 - As a GS Online Banking user on the IMT Transfer details screen, I want to see the amount including any additional fees associated with my international transfer, so that I aware of the Total cost for the transfer.

TC ID	TC Name	Objective	US Ref.	Step No.	Test Step Description	Expected Results
TC_14	Verify Transfer Detail screen_4	To verify the total amount is populated	IMT-15	PREQ	The user has completed all the details on the New International Transfer page and is on the Transfer details screen.	
				Step1	Check the total cost field.	• The value should be auto-populated after the user has entered the amount. • The value of this field is the sum of the amount and the standard international fee. (when the radio button for the "Fees will be deducted from" is selected as "The account above") • The value of this field is equal to the amount. (If the user has selected the fees will be deducted from- The funds, I'm sending radio button) • The user is not able to edit this field.

IMT-16 - As a GS Online Banking user on the IMT Transfer details screen, I want to see the current exchange rate for international transfer with the retrieval time, so that I decide on my transfer based on the exchange rate

TC ID	TC Name	Objective	US Ref.	Step No.	Test Step Description	Expected Results
TC_15	Verify Transfer Detail Screen_5	To verify the current exchange rate is populated from SWIFT	IMT-16	PREQ	The user has completed all the details on the New International Transfer page and is on the Transfer details screen.	
				Step1	Check the current exchange field.	• The value should be auto-populated. • The value of this field should be the same as the current rate from the SWIFT system. • User is not able to edit this field
				Step2	Check the current date-time field.	• The value should be auto-populated. • The value of this field should show the date & time when the exchange rate is retrieved from the SWIFT system. • The date-time should not be **less than 30 mins** from the current online banking server date time. • User is not able to edit this field

IMT-17 - As a GS Online Banking user on the IMT Transfer details screen, I want to see the amount that the beneficiary will receive, so that I aware how much amount beneficiary will receive in their currency.

TC ID	TC Name	Objective	US Ref.	Step No.	Test Step Description	Expected Results
TC_16	Verify Transfer Detail Screen_6	To verify what beneficiary will receive field is populated	IMT-17	PREQ	The user has completed all the details on the New International Transfer page and is on the Transfer details screen.	
				Step1	Check the beneficiary Received field.	• The value should be auto-populated. • The value of this field should be equal to the (Amount x Current rate). • User is not able to edit this field

IMT-18 - As a GS Online Banking user on the IMT Transfer details screen, I want to view the terms and conditions for my international transfer, so that I can acknowledge them.

TC ID	TC Name	Objective	US Ref.	Step No.	Test Step Description	Expected Results
TC_17	Verify Transfer Detail Screen_7	To verify the link for terms and conditions page	IMT-18	PREQ	The user has completed all the details on the New International Transfer page and is on the Transfer details screen.	
				Step1	Check if there is a link for terms and conditions	• There should be a link for the terms and conditions in the Terms and conditions section. • Once user click on the link they are directed to terms and condition page
				Step2	Check the content of the terms and conditions page	The content of terms and conditions should be the same as International Transfer Terms and conditions in the RISK system.
TC_18	Verify Transfer Detail Screen_8	To verify the user can accept terms and conditions	IMT-18	PREQ	The user has completed all the details on the New International Transfer page and is on the Transfer details screen.	By default, the terms and conditions checkbox should not be checked
				Step1	Check the default status of the terms and conditions checkbox	The user can check-in the checkbox and a tick is visible in the box.
				Step2	Try to select the terms and conditions checkbox	The user can check-in the checkbox and a tick is visible in the box.

IMT-19 - As a GS Online Banking user on the IMT Transfer details screen, I want an option to go back to the International Transfer main screen, so that I can modify the previously entered details.

TC ID	TC Name	Objective	US Ref.	Step No.	Test Step Description	Expected Results
TC_19	Verify Transfer Detail screen_9	To verify the user can go back to the new International detail page	IMT-19	PREQ	The user has completed all the details on the New International Transfer page and detail page and is on the Transfer Confirmation screen.	
				Step1	Click on the back button	• The user is transferred to the New International detail page. • All the information entered by the user are retained in the page • User can modify any of the information entered before

IMT-20 - As a GS Online Banking user on the IMT Transfer details screen, I want to proceed to the next screen, so that I can confirm the details entered for the international transfer.

TC ID	TC Name	Objective	US Ref.	Step No.	Test Step Description	Expected Results
TC_20	Verify Transfer Detail screen_10	To verify confirm button functionality in the Transfer detail Page	IMT-20	PREQ	The user has completed all the details on the New International Transfer page and is on the Transfer details screen.	
				Step1	User has entered the valid amount and clicked on the terms and conditions checkbox and clicked on the Next button	The user is landed on the Transfer receipt page.

IMT-21 - As a GS Online Banking user on the IMT Transfer confirmation screen, I want to see the Total amount that will be transferred, so that I confirm the amount before final transfer.

TC ID	TC Name	Objective	US Ref.	Step No.	Test Step Description	Expected Results
TC_21	Verify Transfer Confirm Screen_1	To verify Amount in the Transfer Confirmation Page	IMT-21	PREQ	The user has completed all the details on the New International Transfer page and detail page and is on the Transfer Confirmation screen.	
				Step1	Check the amount displayed in the **amount** field	• The account selected should be the same as the Total amount from the Transfer detail page • The user should not be able to edit the field values

IMT-22 - As a GS Online Banking user on the IMT Transfer confirmation screen, I want to see the selected debit account, so that I confirm the account details before final transfer.

TC ID	TC Name	Objective	US Ref.	Step No.	Test Step Description	Expected Results
TC_22	Verify Transfer Confirm Screen_2	To verify From Account in the Transfer Confirmation Page	IMT-22	PREQ	The user has completed all the details on the New International Transfer page and detail page and is on the Transfer Confirmation screen.	
				Step1	Check the account displayed in the **from account** field	• The account selected should be the same as the account selected on the Transfer main page • The user should not be able to edit the field values

IMT-23 - As a GS Online Banking user on the IMT Transfer confirmation screen, I want to see the beneficiary account, so that I confirm the beneficiary account details before final transfer

TC ID	TC Name	Objective	US Ref.	Step No.	Test Step Description	Expected Results
TC_23	Verify Transfer Confirm Screen_3	To verify To Account in the Transfer Confirmation Page	IMT-23	PREQ	The user has completed all the details on the New International Transfer page and detail page and is on the Transfer Confirmation screen.	
				Step1	Check the account displayed in the **beneficiary account** field	• The account selected should be the same as the beneficiary account from the Transfer main page • The user should not be able to edit the field values

IMT-24 - As a GS Online Banking user on the IMT Transfer confirmation screen, I want to see the payment date & disclaimer, so that I am aware when the beneficiary will receive the payment.

TC ID	TC Name	Objective	US Ref.	Step No.	Test Step Description	Expected Results
TC_24	Verify Transfer Confirm Screen_4	To verify the Payment Date & disclaimer in the Transfer Confirmation Page	IMT-24	PREQ	The user has completed all the details on the New International Transfer page and detail page and is on the Transfer Confirmation screen.	
				Step1	Check the date displayed in the payment date field	• The date should be displayed as the current system date from RISK system + 2-3 business days • User should not be able to edit the field values
				Step2	Check the disclaimer after the payment date	The disclaimer should be "It takes 2-3 business days to process international transfers Important: Please check that the account details are correct. We may not be able to recover funds sent to the wrong account."

IMT-25 - As a GS Online Banking user on the IMT Confirmation screen, I want an option to go back to the International Transfer detail screen, so that I can modify the previously entered details.

TC ID	TC Name	Objective	US Ref.	Step No.	Test Step Description	Expected Results
TC_25	Verify Transfer Confirm Screen_5	To verify back button functionality in the Transfer Confirmation Page	IMT-25	PREQ	The user has completed all the details on the New International Transfer page and detail page and is on the Transfer Confirmation screen.	
				Step1	Click on the back button	• The user is on the Transfer detail page. • All the information entered by the user are retained on the page • User can modify any of the information entered before

IMT-26 - As a GS Online Banking user on the IMT Transfer Confirmation screen, I want to proceed to the next screen, so that I can confirm the details entered for the international transfer

TC ID	TC Name	Objective	US Ref.	Step No.	Test Step Description	Expected Results
TC_26	Verify Transfer Confirm Screen_6	To verify confirm button functionality in the Transfer Confirmation Page	IMT-26	PREQ	The user has completed all the details on the New International Transfer page and transfer details screen and is currently on the Confirmation page.	
				Step1	The user clicked on the Confirm button.	The user is landed on the Transfer receipt page.

IMT-27 - As a GS Online Banking user on the Transfer Receipt screen, I want to see the final transfer details, so that I can keep the receipt for my records.

TC ID	TC Name	Objective	US Ref.	Step No.	Test Step Description	Expected Results
TC_27	Verify Transfer Receipt Screen_1	To verify the values on Transfer Receipt Page	IMT-27	PREQ	The user has completed all the details on the New International Transfer page and detail page and confirmed the payment on the confirmation page	The user is currently on the Transfer receipt page
				Step1	Check the fields on the Receipt page	• Requested on, Amount, updated balance, From, To and the payment date is the same as the previous pages. • User should not be able to edit the field values

IMT-28 - As a GS Online Banking user on the Transfer Receipt screen, I want to see a receipt number for my transfer, so that I can use it for tracking the transfer

TC ID	TC Name	Objective	US Ref.	Step No.	Test Step Description	Expected Results
TC_28	Verify Transfer Receipt Screen_2	To verify the receipt number on Transfer Receipt Page	IMT-28	PREQ	The user has completed all the details on the New International Transfer page and detail page and confirmed the payment on the confirmation page	The user is currently on the Transfer receipt page
				Step1	Check the receipt number displayed	• The field is a 12-digit alphanumeric field • The user should not be able to edit the field values

IMT-29 - As a GS Online Banking user on the Transfer Receipt screen, I want to have an option to print the confirmation details, so that I keep a receipt of transfer for tracking and future reference

TC ID	TC Name	Objective	US Ref.	Step No.	Test Step Description	Expected Results
TC_29	Verify Transfer Receipt Screen_3	To verify the print functionality on Transfer Receipt Page	IMT-29	PREQ	The user has completed all the details on the New International Transfer page and detail page and confirmed the payment on the confirmation page	The user is currently on the Transfer receipt page
				Step1	Click on the print button	The print window is displayed to select the printer

IMT-30 - As a GS Online Banking user on the IMT main screen, I want to see an appropriate error message if the entered account number or IBAN is invalid, so that I can modify it before the transfer

TC ID	TC Name	Objective	US Ref.	Step No.	Test Step Description	Expected Results
TC_30	Verify IMT Main Screen Error Hand_1	To verify the user is shown an appropriate error message if the account number and IBAN are invalid and the user can't proceed to the next screen	IMT-30	PREQ	The user has clicked on the "New International Transfer" menu and is on the New International Transfer page	
				Step1	User complete all the mandatory fields in the Transfer main screen and enter invalid account number e.g. 000000 or 1234 (less than six digits)	• The account number or IBAN field is highlighted in red with an exclamation sign in the end. • Error message "Account number or IBAN is invalid. Please try again." is displayed below the field. • The user stays on the "New international transfer" screen
				Step2	User complete all the mandatory fields in the Transfer main screen and enter invalid IBAN code, e.g., xxx232343, and click on next button	• The account number or IBAN field is highlighted in red with an exclamation sign at the end. • Error message "Account number or IBAN is invalid. Please try again." is displayed below the field. • The user stays on the "New international transfer" screen

IMT-31 - As a GS Online Banking user on the IMT main screen, I want to see an appropriate error message if the entered SWIFT code is invalid, so that I can modify it before the transfer

TC ID	TC Name	Objective	US Ref.	Step No.	Test Step Description	Expected Results
TC_31	Verify IMT Main Screen Error Hand_2	To verify the user is shown an appropriate error message if the SWIFT code is invalid and the user can't proceed to the next screen	IMT-31	PREQ	The user has clicked on the "New International Transfer" menu and is on the New International Transfer page	
				Step1	The user completes all the mandatory fields in the Transfer main screen and enters an invalid SWIFT code. E.g., TEST123	• The SWIFT code field is highlighted in red with an exclamation sign at the end. • Error message "SWIFT code is invalid. Please try again. "is displayed below the field. • The user stays on the "**New international transfer**" screen

IMT-32 - As a GS Online Banking user on the IMT Transfer details screen, I want to see an appropriate error message if I have entered amount which is not in the range specified by the bank, so that I can modify the amount to be in range.

TC ID	TC Name	Objective	US Ref.	Step No.	Test Step Description	Expected Results
TC_32	Verify Transfer Detail Screen Error Hand_3	To verify bank minimum and maximum limit is enforced for user input amount field	IMT-32	PREQ	The user has completed all the details on the New International Transfer page and is on the Transfer details screen.	
				Step1	Check the min and max limit for international transfer in RISK	The min limit is $10 and max limit is set as $10,000 ***If the min and max limit is changed by bank this test case need to be updated to reflect this.**
				Step2	User entered amount as 9.99 (value exactly before the boundary value of 10)	• The Amount field is highlighted in red with an exclamation sign in the end • Error message "Amount less than the minimum limit. Please try again." is displayed below the field • User stays on the "Transfer Detail" screen
				Step3	User entered amount as 10.00 (value exactly at the boundary value of 10)	• There is no error message displayed • The user is landed on the Transfer confirmation page
				Step4	User entered amount as 10.01 (value above the boundary value of 10)	• There is no error message displayed • The user is landed on the Transfer confirmation page.
				Step5	User entered amount as 9999.99 (value exactly before the boundary value of 10,000)	• There is no error message displayed • The user is landed on the Transfer confirmation page.
				Step6	User entered amount as 10,000 (value exactly at the boundary value of 10,000)	• There is no error message displayed • The user is landed on the Transfer confirmation page.
				Step7	User entered amount as 10,000.01 (value above the boundary value of 10,000)	• The Amount field is highlighted in red with an exclamation sign at the end. • Error message "Amount greater than the maximum limit. Please try again." is displayed below the field. • The user stays on the "Transfer Detail" screen

IMT-33 - As a GS Online Banking user on the IMT Transfer details screen, I want to see an appropriate error message if the total cost is greater than my account balance, so that I can change the transfer amount.

TC ID	TC Name	Objective	US Ref.	Step No.	Test Step Description	Expected Results
TC_33	Verify Transfer Detail Screen Error Hand_4	To verify that the user can proceed if the total amount is greater than the account balance	IMT-33	PREQ	The user has completed all the details on the New International Transfer page and is on the Transfer details screen.	
				Step1	Total cost is 1 cent less than the amount balance (value exactly before the boundary value), e.g., if the balance is $100 and the total amount calculated based on the input is $99.99.	• There is no error message displayed • The user is landed on the Transfer confirmation page.
				Step2	User entered amount equal to the account balance (value exactly at the boundary value)	• There is no error message displayed • The user is landed on the Transfer confirmation page.
				Step3	Total cost is 1 cent more than the amount balance (value exactly above the boundary value), e.g., if the balance is $100 and the total amount calculated based on the input is $100.01.	• The Amount field is highlighted in red with an exclamation sign at the end. • Error message "Amount greater than the Account balance. Please try again." is displayed below the field. • The user stays on the "Transfer Detail" screen

IMT-34 - As a GS Online Banking user on the IMT Transfer details screen, I want to see an appropriate error message if I have missed to enter any of the mandatory detail, so that I can enter them now.

TC ID	TC Name	Objective	US Ref.	Step No.	Test Step Description	Expected Results
TC_34	Verify Transfer Detail Screen Error Hand_5	To verify that the user cannot proceed to the transfer confirmation page unless they have completed all mandatory fields on the Transfer detail page	IMT-34	PREQ	The user has completed all the details on the New International Transfer page and is on the Transfer details screen.	
				Step1	The user has not entered the amount and not checked in the terms and conditions checkbox and clicked on the Next button	• I have read terms and conditions and the amount field is highlighted in red with exclamation sign in the end. • Error message "Please agree to the terms and conditions." is displayed below the terms and conditions field in red. • Error message "Please enter the amount and try again." is displayed below the field in red. • User stays on the "Transfer Detail" screen
				Step2	The user has not entered the amount but has checked in the terms and conditions checkbox and clicked on the Next button	• The Amount field is highlighted in red with an exclamation sign in the end. • Error message "Please enter the amount and try again." is displayed below the field. • User stays on the "Transfer Detail" screen

IMT-35 - As a GS Online Banking user on the IMT Transfer details screen, I want to see an appropriate error message if I have not acknowledged the terms and conditions for the transfer, so that I read and acknowledge them.

TC ID	TC Name	Objective	US Ref.	Step No.	Test Step Description	Expected Results
TC_35	Verify Transfer Detail Screen Error Hand_6	To verify that the user cannot proceed to the transfer confirmation page unless terms and conditions is acknowledged	IMT-35	PREQ	The user has completed all the details on the New International Transfer page and is on the Transfer details screen.	
				Step1	User has entered the amount but not checked in the terms and conditions checkbox and clicked on the Next button	• I have read the terms and conditions, and the amount field is highlighted in red with an exclamation sign at the end. • Error message "Please agree to the terms and conditions. "is displayed below the terms and conditions field in red. • The user stays on the "Transfer Detail" screen

IMT-36 - As a GS Online Banking user who has completed an international transfer, I want to receive the receipt of my transfer to my email, which I have provided to the bank, so that I can use that for tracking and future reference.

TC ID	TC Name	Objective	US Ref.	Step No.	Test Step Description	Expected Results
TC_36	Verify Transfer Receipt mail_1	To verify the user receives the new confirmation mail after the International fund transfer	IMT-36	PREQ	The user has completed all the details on the New International Transfer page and detail page and confirmed the payment on the confirmation page	The user is currently on the Transfer receipt page
				Step1	Check the new mail is there for the user as a confirmation	• The user received a new mail in the mailbox • The new mail should have all the details similar to the confirmation page

IMT-37 - As a GS Online Banking user who has completed an international transfer, I want to receive the receipt of my transfer as a notification to my internet banking mailbox, so that I can use that for tracking and future reference.

TC ID	TC Name	Objective	US Ref.	Step No.	Test Step Description	Expected Results
TC_37	Verify Transfer Receipt mail_2	To verify the user receives the new confirmation mail after the International fund transfer	IMT-37	PREQ	The user has completed all the details on the New International Transfer page and detail page and confirmed the payment on the confirmation page	The user is currently on the Transfer receipt page
				Step1	Check the new mail is there for the user as a confirmation	• The user received a new mail in the internet banking mailbox • The new mail should have all the details similar to the confirmation page

IMT-38 - As a GS Online Banking user who has completed an international transfer, my account balance must be updated, so that I am aware of my current balance immediately after the transfer.

TC ID	TC Name	Objective	US Ref.	Step No.	Test Step Description	Expected Results
TC_38	Verify Transfer Account balance	To verify the user account balance is updated after International fund transfer	IMT-38	PREQ	User has completed International Transfer page	
				Step1	Check the balance of Account used for transfer on Account summary page	• The account balance should be updated to reflect the transfer • In the account transactions there should be a new transaction for transfer

IMT-39 - As a GS Online Banking user, the beneficiary country for bank location or address should be checked against the latest backlist country list before the final transfer, so that I know my transfer will be successful.

TC ID	TC Name	Objective	US Ref.	Step No.	Test Step Description	Expected Results
TC_39	Verify_ blacklist country_1	To verify the user can't proceed if the beneficiary country for bank location or address is blacklisted	IMT-39	PREQ	• User has selected the beneficiary country for bank location or address and currently on transfer detail page. • Selected country is now blacklisted in RISK system.	
				Step1	User click on the next button	• Error message "Please change the beneficiary country for bank location or address field" is displayed in red. • The user stays on the "Transfer Detail" screen.
TC_40	Verify_ blacklist country_2	To verify the user can't complete transfer if the beneficiary country for bank location or address is blacklisted	IMT-39	PREQ	• User has selected the beneficiary country for bank location or address and currently on transfer confirmation page. • Selected country is now blacklisted in RISK system.	
				Step1	User click on the confirm button	• Error message "Please change the beneficiary country for bank location or address field" is displayed in red. • The user stays on the "Transfer Confirmation" screen.

Note
In the Agile projects, generally, the software delivery to the customer is done in increments, i.e., features are delivered one by one to the customer, especially if time-to-market is important. As IMT project is a complex, high-risk banking project, the team has decided to deliver all the features in one go rather than in increments. This will allow the a full-fledge end-to-end testing of the system after the end of all the sprints.

Note
In the Agile projects, the focus is to complete the stories that are part of the Sprint. In this process, the development team does shortcuts in the code or creates low-quality code or temporary hacks in quick fixing or skipping automation of tests. These hacks can create technical debt (also known as design debt or code debt) for the team. Some of the teams leave the defects for future sprints, which also form some type of technical debt —these technical debt results in an implied cost of additional rework, which needs to be done later.   Refactoring is a disciplined way to restructure code to remove technical debts. It simplifies the design of code without altering its behavior to increase maintainability and readability. Teams refactor code before adding updates or releasing features to improve code quality so that future iterations built on original code are not bogged down by confusion and clutter. Refactoring enables the Agile team to evolve the code slowly over time, to take an iterative and incremental approach to implementation.   To resolve any lingering defects and other forms of technical debts, the team may use "hardening" or "stabilization" iterations between the regular iterations. These iterations can be shorter than the standard sprint size (1 week) and help the team eliminate any technical debts and lingering defects.

18 **End to End testing**

For the IMT project, once all the iterations are completed, the testing team will do end-to-end testing to ensure that the system works end to end from the user's perspective. This should ensure a successful integration of all the features and continuity between components developed by different teams. This testing will often identify gaps that are difficult to discover inside agile teams, including flows across the product. Generally, in most projects, this testing is done by a separate testing team (testers who were not involved in sprint testing). This approach seeks to encourage an independent mindset to compliment the testing done during the sprints. This independent testing team may add more tests to make sure all the end-to-end functionality is covered.

Note
In parallel to end-to-end testing, some other non-functional testing like usability, security, performance testing will be done for the IMT project. Generally, some level of this non-functional testing is done in Agile projects when the stories are developed during the sprints. They may also be tracked as separate stories covering non-functional attributes for the system.
After the end-to-end testing is completed, regression testing will be done to ensure the new IMT changes have not impacted any existing functionality. IMT Regression testing will verify that the IMT code changes have not introduced any new defects in the existing online banking system. Impact Analysis is performed to find which of the existing functionality may be impacted due to the changes; based on this information, the test cases are selected from the existing Regression Test suite.

The following pages show the system's end-to-end flow during E2E testing with all the relevant error messages.

Global Sun Online Banking Login Page

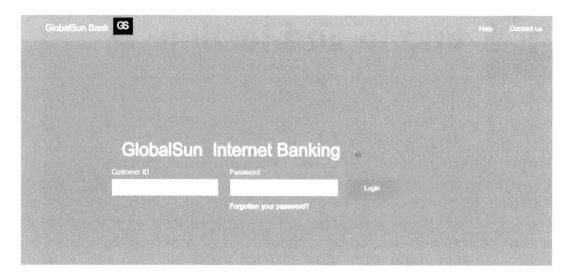

User enter the valid Customer ID and password and click on the Login button

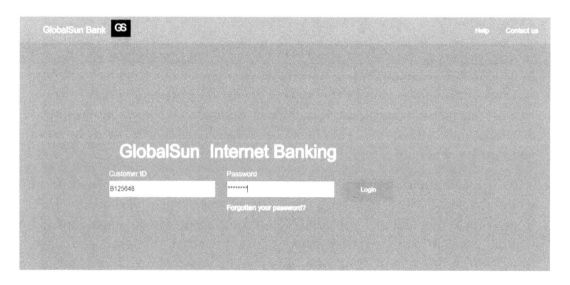

After successful login user is transferred to the Account Summary page

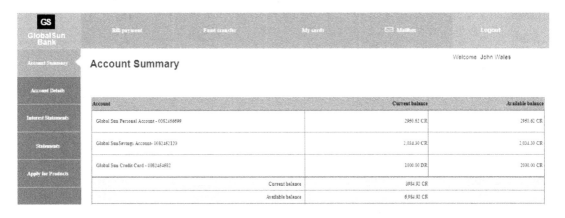

User can see the Account details for their different accounts

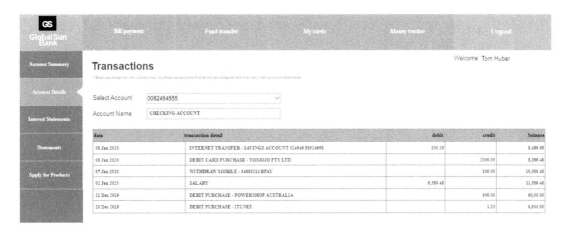

User not entitled to International transfer cannot see the "New International transfer" menu under Fund transfer

User entitled for International transfer can see the "New International transfer" menu under Fund transfer

Once the user selects the "New International transfer" menu from Fund Transfer, they are transferred to the New International transfer main page

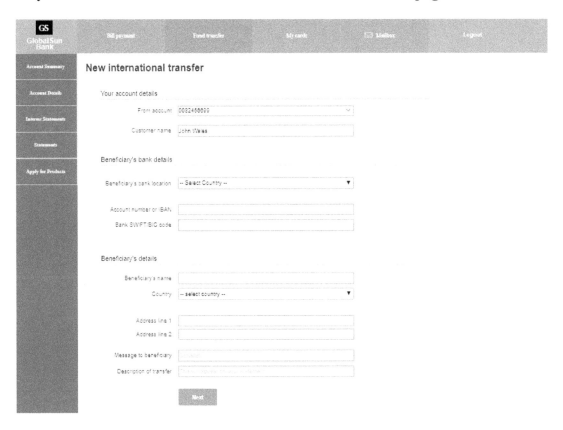

If the user enters the wrong Account number or IBAN and clicks on the Next button, an error message is displayed

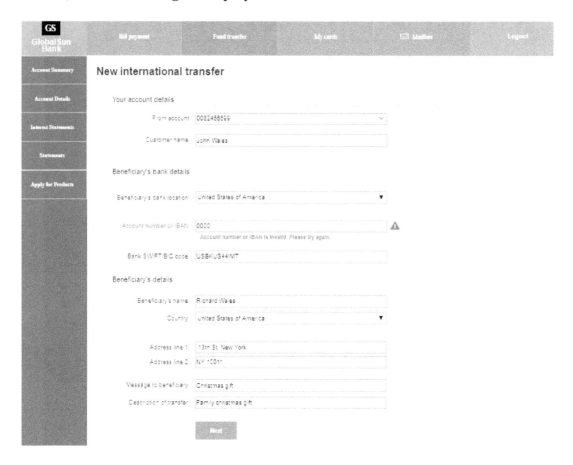

If the user enters an invalid Bank SWIFT/BIC code and clicks on the Next button, an error message is displayed

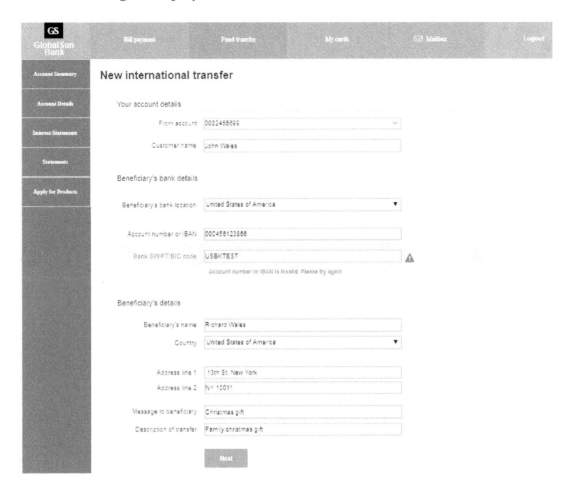

After the user fill all mandatory fields on Transfer main page and click on the Next button, they are transferred to the Transfer Detail page

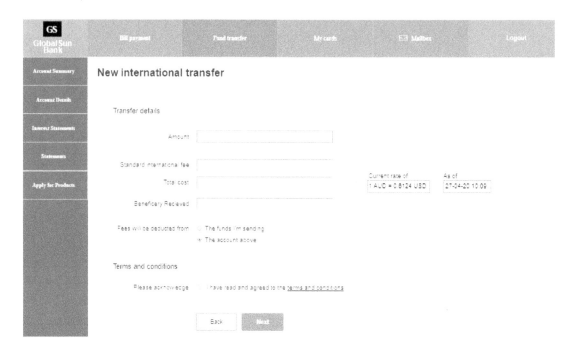

User click on terms and conditions link, and a new popup window is displayed

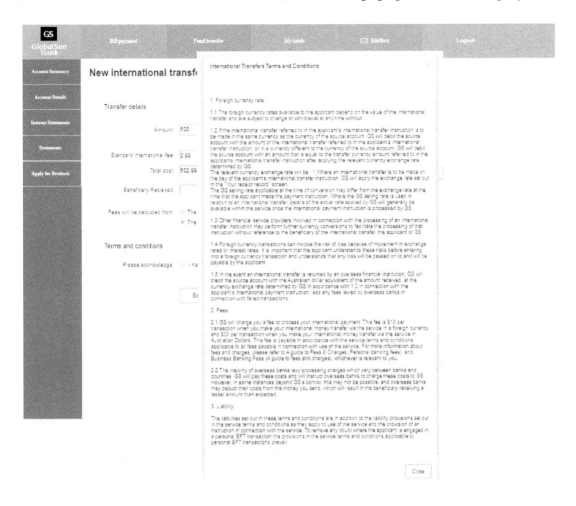

If the User enter Amount more than transfer limit and click on Next button, an error message is displayed

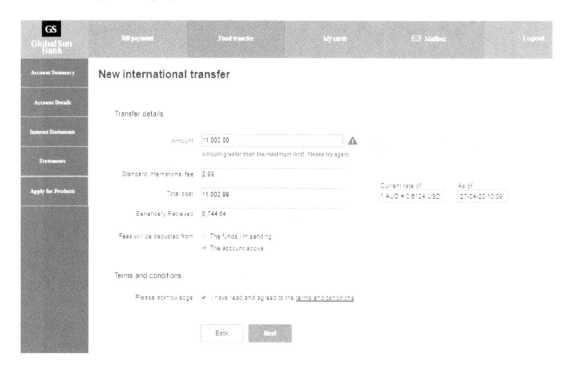

If the user enters an amount less than the minimum limit for International transfer and clicks on the Next button, an error message is displayed

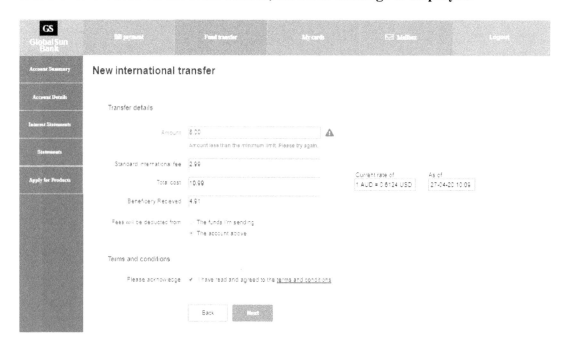

If the user leaves the amount field blank and clicks on the Next button, error message is displayed

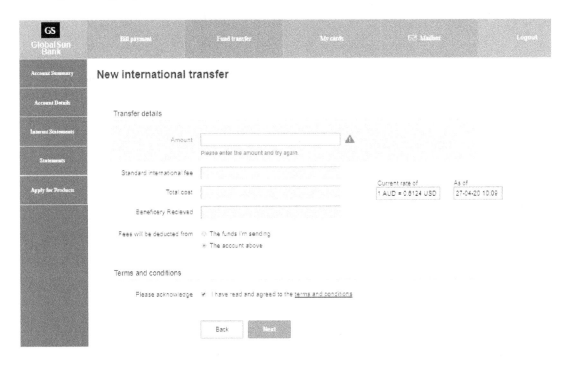

After the user enter all the mandatory fields in Transfer Detail page and clicks on the Next button, they are transferred to the Transfer confirmation page

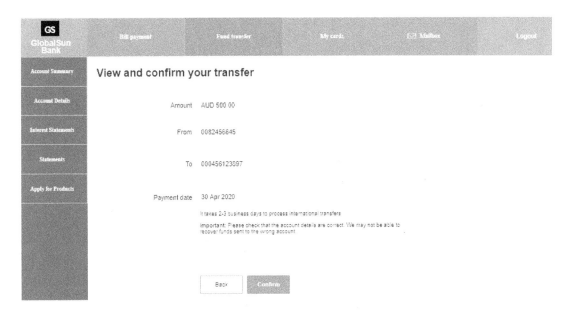

Once the user clicks on the confirm button, they are transferred to the Transfer Receipt page, with a new message in the Mailbox

After the User click on the Mailbox menu and select the new mail, the receipt for transfer is displayed

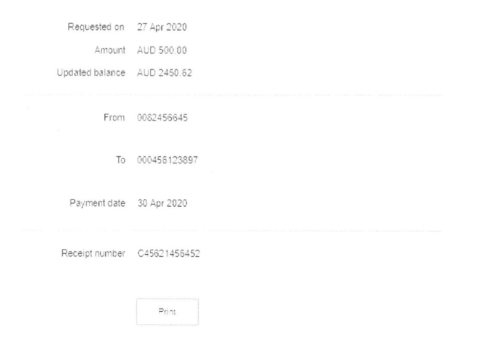

19   **UAT Testing**

As we have discussed earlier, some level of UAT testing is done by the Product Owner and business SME's during the sprint after user story testing. Still, after all the development is complete, an end-to-end UAT cycle is run in most organizations, which focuses on the behavior and capabilities of a whole system or product. Objectives of this acceptance testing include:

- Establishing confidence in the quality of the system as a whole
- Validating that the system is complete and will work as expected
- Verifying that functional and non-functional behaviors of the system are as specified

Acceptance testing may produce information to assess the system's readiness for deployment and use by the customer (end-user). Defects may be found during acceptance testing, but finding defects is often not an objective, and finding a significant number of defects during acceptance testing may, in some cases, be considered a major project risk. Acceptance testing may also satisfy legal or regulatory requirements or standards.

The test team may support the UAT testing as the business users are sometimes unaware of the overall UAT test process and testing tools used to support this testing. Examples include helping the UAT business testers to raise defects in defect tracking tools, assisting them in preparing test status reports and UAT environment shakedown tests.

UAT is performed in the UAT test environment (different from the system test environment), similar to the real operational production environment with similar test data. These factors help find some of the defects that can be replicated in a production-like environment and data.

The UAT for IMT will focus on end-to-end positive test scenarios to validate that the new IMT system is complete and working as expected.

<table>
<tr><td>**20**</td><td># Recap & Next steps</td></tr>
</table>

After going through all the topics, I believe you should be now clear with the Agile software development life cycle and how testing is done in the Agile projects. The following diagram provides a quick recap of different Scrum ceremonies, different scrum team members, and how testers collaborate with these team members for the testing activities.

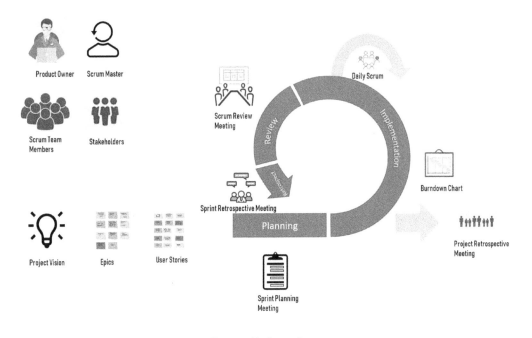

Sprint Lifecycle

Looking at the above diagram, check your understanding of each ceremony's value, purpose, and tester's contribution to each of them and how different testing activities are done during a sprint. If you are confident to participate in these ceremonies and perform the Agile tester tasks, you have earned yourself the title of **"Self-Taught Agile Software Tester."**

Based on the knowledge you have gained from the book, you are ready to work on an Agile project that will enable you to gain some real-time work experience. The activities learned in the book can be implemented for a variety of projects.

I will suggest you brush up on all the topics discussed in this book, learn and explore more topics on Agile from other sources, and check your understanding with other folks who work in Agile software development. This all will help you in your interview preparation. As there is a lot of emphasis on automation and API testing in Agile projects, it is worth sharpening your skills in these areas by learning the tools used for automation and API testing. You may also try to get certified on your Agile testing skills through The International Software Testing Qualifications Board (ISTQB). For more details, check out https://www.istqb.org/

Most large organizations still follow the hybrid model for development, where some of the projects run in Agile and other use sequential development. If you don't have any exposure to sequential development, you can also refer to my book, **"The Self-Taught Software Tester."** This book covers the same IMT project using the sequential development methodology.

I hope this book will help you prepare for your interview and guide you in your future testing career. All the best.

21 | **Glossary of terms**

Term	Definition
Acceptance criteria	The criteria that a component or system must satisfy in order to be accepted by a user, customer, or other authorized entity.
Agile Manifesto	A statement on the values that underpin Agile software development. The values are individuals and interactions over processes and tools, working software over comprehensive documentation, customer collaboration over contract negotiation, responding to change over following a plan.
Agile software development	A group of software development methodologies based on iterative incremental development, where requirements and solutions evolve through collaboration between self-organizing cross- functional teams.
Behavior-driven development (BDD)	Behavior-driven development (BDD) is an Agile software development process that encourages collaboration among developers, testers and business participants. It encourages teams to use conversation and concrete examples to formalize a shared understanding of how the application should behave. BDD tool can be used to automate these examples.
Build verification test	A set of automated tests which validates the integrity of each new build and verifies its key/core functionality, stability and testability.
Exploratory testing	An approach to testing whereby the testers dynamically design and execute tests based on their knowledge, exploration of the test item and the results of previous tests.
Incremental development model	A type of software development lifecycle model in which the component or system is developed through a series of increments.
Iterative development model	A type of software development lifecycle model in which the component or system is developed through a series of repeated cycles.
Minimum Viable Product MVP	A minimum viable product (MVP) is a version of a product with just enough features to be usable by early customers who can then provide feedback for future product development.

Test approach	The implementation of the test strategy for a specific project.
Test Automation	The use of software to perform or support test activities, e.g., test management, test design, test execution and results checking.
Test basis	The body of knowledge used as the basis for test analysis and design.
Test charter	Documentation of test activities in session-based exploratory testing.
Test-driven development (TDD)	A way of developing software where the test cases are developed, and often automated, before the coding of the software.
Test estimation	The calculated approximation of a result related to various aspects of testing (e.g., effort spent, completion date, costs involved, number of test cases, etc.) which is usable even if input data may be incomplete, uncertain, or noisy
Test execution automation	The use of software, e.g., capture/playback tools, to control the execution of tests, the comparison of actual results to expected results, the setting up of test preconditions, and other test control and reporting functions.
Test oracle	A source to determine an expected result to compare with the actual result of the system under test.
Test strategy	Documentation that expresses the generic requirements for testing one or more projects run within an organization, providing detail on how testing is to be performed, and is aligned with the test policy.
Quality risk	A product risk related to a quality characteristic.
Regression testing	Testing of a previously tested component or system following modification to ensure that defects have not been introduced or have been uncovered in unchanged areas of the software, as a result of the changes made.
Software lifecycle	The use of software to perform or support test activities, e.g., test management, test design, test execution and results checking.
Unit test framework	A tool that provides an environment for unit or component testing in which a component can be tested in isolation or with suitable stubs and drivers. It also provides other support for the developer, such as debugging capabilities
User story	A user or business requirement consisting of one sentence expressed in the everyday or business language, which is capturing the functionality a user needs, the reason behind it, any non-functional criteria, and also including acceptance criteria.

www.ingramcontent.com/pod-product-compliance
Lightning Source LLC
LaVergne TN
LVHW081343050326
832903LV00024B/1288